Juvenile Justice in Rural America

The United States Department of Justice

Law Enforcement Assistance Administration

Office of Juvenile Justice and Delinquency Prevention

For sale by the Superintendent of Documents, U.S. Government Printing Office, Washington, D.C. 20402

JUVENILE JUSTICE IN RURAL AMERICA

Edited by

Joanne Jankovic, Assistant Professor
University of Tennessee School of Social Work
Knoxville, Tennessee

Ronald K. Green, Director
Office of Continuing Social Work Education
University of Tennessee School of Social Work
Knoxville, Tennessee

Shanler D. Cronk, Assistant Attorney General
State of Nebraska
Lincoln, Nebraska

This project was supported by Grant Number 0-0201-J-LEAA awarded by the Law Enforcement Assistance Administration, U.S. Department of Justice, under the Omnibus Crime Control and Safe Streets Act of 1968, as amended. Points of view or opinions stated in this document are those of the authors and do not necessarily represent the official position or policies of the U.S. Department of Justice.

ISBN 0-89695-005-0

TABLE OF CONTENTS

CONTRIBUTORS

DAVID W. BROWN is International Professor of Agricultural Economics and Rural Sociology at the University of Tennessee, Knoxville.

KRISTIN N. CHAMBERS, MSW, is a graduate of West Virginia University and a resident of Dunbar, West Virginia.

STEPHEN DAHL is a Social Worker in the Waushara County Department of Social Services, Wautoma, Wisconsin.

JOSEPH DEJAMES is Director, Detention Monitoring Unit, New Jersey Department of Corrections, Trenton, New Jersey.

EDMUND T. DIMOCK, MSW, ACSW, is Program Supervisor, Youth Crisis Services, Children's Home Society of California, Northern District, Chico.

MORRIS A. FORSLUND, PhD, is Professor of Sociology, University of Wyoming Laramie.

JOANNE JANKOVIC, MSW, is Assistant Professor at the University of Tennessee School of Social Work, Knoxville Branch.

H. WAYNE JOHNSON is Professor at the University of Iowa School of Social Work, Iowa City.

KEVIN W. LAWLESS is Director of the Tri-town Council on Youth and Family Services, Topsfield, Massachusetts.

KENNETH LIBERTOFF, PhD, is a private consultant in matters of juvenile justice and a resident of Montpelier, Vermont.

EDWIN J. MINER, MSW, is a graduate of West Virginia University and a resident of Dunbar, West Virginia.

EDWARD J. PAWLAK, PhD, is Professor at Western Michigan University, School of Social Work, Kalamazoo.

GEORGIANNA SHEPARD is Assistant Professor, Department of Sociology, University of Wisconsin, Superior, Wisconsin.

JOHN R. WARNER, JR. is Associate Professor in the Department of Sociology, West Virginia Wesleyan College, Buckhannon, West Virginia.

PREFACE

The genesis of this publication is found in the concern of a number of persons that the major focus of federal justice policy has been understandably urban. As a result, a certain vacuum has been created in regard to the clear identification of rural justice issues and the gathering of usable information as to how those issues can best be addressed.

The National Rural Center first initiated a response to this vacuum in planning an invitational conference, "A Beginning Assessment of the Justice System in Rural America" held in Austin, Texas, October, 1977. One of the results of this effort was pressure to hold an open conference on rural justice in an attempt to identify and link those from various disciplines who are currently working on rural justice issues. Based on this pressure, the National Rural Center contacted the University of Tennessee School of Social Work's Office of Continuing Social Work Education to help initiate such a conference which resulted in the National Symposium on Rural Justice held June 20-22, 1979, in Knoxville, Tennessee.

Recognizing that one of the problems in the rural justice field was a lack of organized literature, the symposium was planned with the thought of organizing papers prepared for presentation into a series of publications dealings with rural justice. This publication and a companion publication, Criminal Justice in Rural America, supported by the National Institute of Justice, represent this effort.

The juvenile justice papers available from the symposium were reviewed to identify those dealing with issues, current changes, program responses or planning models for the future. Where these were not available from the symposium, the literature was reviewed to secure papers already available and/or potential authors were asked to produce relevant material on the subject needed. Thus, this publication draws together the current "state of the art" in rural juvenile justice with the objective of providing an initial attempt at producing an organized body of literature in this area.

The material in this book has been organized in a logical sequence of identifying current issues through a review of current research in the area; identifying those forces causing changes in the current systems; reviewing a broad number of program responses to rural juvenile justice problems; and providing planning models on which current and future decision making regarding rural juvenile justice can be based.

Each major section is prefaced by an introductory statement which provides a review of the material contained therein and should enable the reader to locate specific material when required.

This book is not seen as the final statement in rural juvenile justice but rather as an initial statement, hopefully as a stimulus to others, to help organize the literature in this field so it can be available to help influence the shape of rural juvenile justice policy and programming in the decade to follow.

ACKNOWLEDGMENTS

The effort required to plan and execute a national symposium and to produce a usable publication as a result can only be generated by the total work of a large number of persons. Although the editors were involved from the beginning, it was only through the support provided by our respective organizations and the many cooperating organizations that this publication is made possible.

Appreciation is given to the strong support provided by Ben P. Granger, Dean of the University of Tennessee School of Social Work, and Jack Cornman, President of the National Rural Center, who provided the organizational backing necessary to carry off the symposium and initiate this publication.

In addition to the editors, the symposium planning committee consisted of Gideon Fryer and Richard Edwards of the University of Tennessee School of Social Work, Curtis Wells of the University of Tennessee College of Law, David Brown of the University of Tennessee Department of Agricultural Economics and Rural Sociology, Stephen Webster of the University of Wisconsin School of Social Work and Joanne Pozo of the National Resource Center for Consumers of Legal Services. We thank those members for their dedicated efforts in planning the symposium and providing the vehicle for this publication.

No publication is possible without a great deal of professional work by editorial staff who provide the technical publication work. Much thanks is given to Sally Johnson, publications editor for the Office of Continuing Social Work Education, and her staff: Ann Wilson, JoAnna Cheatham, Joyce Payne and Pamela Jones.

Acknowledgment is given to the following for use of copyrighted materials:

SOCIAL WELFARE IN APPALACHIA for "Juvenile Justice in West Virginia: A Changing Landscape," by Kristin N. Chambers and Edwin J. Miner.

Baywood Publishing Company, Inc., "Drug Use and Delinquent Behavior of Small Town and Rural Youth," by Morris A. Forslund.

CHILD WELFARE for "Youth Crisis Services: Short-Term Community-Based Residential Treatment," by Edmund T. Dimock

Haworth Press, Inc., for "Educational Justice for Children in Rural/Nonmetroplitan Areas," by Joanne Jankovic.

H. Wayne Johnson for "Crime, Delinquency and Criminal Justice in Rural America."

Kenneth Libertoff for "The Runaway Youth Issue: Implications for Rural Communities."

Edward J. Pawlak for "Juvenile Justice: A Rural-Urban Comparison."

Finally, we acknowledge the critical support provided by the Federal Office of Juvenile Justice and Delinquency Prevention who have provided the necessary support that enabled us to bring this publication from merely an idea into actuality.

PART I

RURAL JUVENILE JUSTICE: EXPLORING THE ISSUES

Introduction

Generally, little is known about the status of the juvenile justice system in rural America. However, considering the unique characteristics of rural areas, one could surmise that local practices would differ from those in most urban areas, in that: (1) the volume of delinquency activity tends to be less; (2) types of offenses differ due to rurality and economic make-up of an area; (3) local police agencies, courts and community resources would be less formalized than metropolitan areas; and (4) based on available dispositional resources, judicial decision-making patterns differ from jurisdiction to jurisdiction.

Additionally, due to increased emphasis by the federal government on developing and upgrading local law enforcement and court practices, certain issues arise which have considerable implications for many rural/nonmetropolitan communities. First, the quest for uniformity and consistency in practices and better reporting usually requires the development of new programs or an increase in the formalization of certain agency services such as adding special juvenile aid bureaus to existing police departments or creating specialized court intake units. For a rural community, this becomes a costly endeavor because design of programs which usually have urban origins cost more on a per capita basis.

Second, the mandate for new programs and practices often does not take into consideration the local nature of delinquency activity or needs of children in a particular area. For instance, legislative reforms which require that children no longer be held in adult jails or lock-up facilities usually result in the development of a system of juvenile detention facilities. However, such facilities may not be actually needed in a particular area because most delinquency activity may be of a non-serious nature. Moreover, the true need may be for a regional shelter for children with family problems, which does not necessarily require the intervention of juvenile justice agencies.

Readings in the chapters that follow serve a twofold purpose. First, we have attempted to acquaint the reader with a thorough discussion of issues affecting the delivery of rural juvenile justice services, both from a policy and programmatic perspective. Second, we have identified past and present research attempts which identify rural/urban differences in delinquency activity and how these problems are treated comparatively.

Joseph DeJames discusses the particular issues which affect rural programming for juveniles. Considering the various elements which constitute the juvenile justice system--police, courts, probation and dispositional alternatives--he notes the difficulty in implementing urban-oriented standards in rural areas. These issues are discussed in consideration of geographic areas served by rural justice agencies as opposed to population density. For instance, the unit of juvenile justice administration is the county--2,463 of the nation's 3,099 counties are outside Standard Metropolitan Statistical Areas. Thirty-one to 42 percent of this country's citizens live in rural/nonmetropolitan areas. This represents approximately 89 percent of the total area of the United States.

DeJames suggests there are several explanations for lower juvenile arrest rates in rural areas: generally, there is less crime, more stable populations, less alienation and more controls exerted by community institutions. Additionally, there are less opportunities for certain crimes, and fewer persons are apprehended for actual crimes committed.

Also, in certain rural areas, the majority of juvenile crimes are committed not by rural residents, but by their urban counterparts. Last, DeJames discusses the implications of certain major juvenile justice policy issues as they affect rural areas, particularly separation of adult and juvenile offenders in pre-dispositional care facilities.

John Warner presents an historical overview of research into rural crime and delinquency during the period 1930-1979, and offers suggestions for future research. He distinguishes between "rural" and "small town" crime and notes there are distinct differences in the types of crime reported for each area. Crimes which are reported most often in rural areas are offenses against family and children, fraud, manslaughter by negligence and driving while intoxicated. He notes that manslaughter is more often due to traffic deaths and hunting accidents--this is related to location rather than residence. With particular regard to rural delinquency, Warner reported the research suggests delinquent behavior among rural youths develops late in their youth, and gangs are not significant factors in rural juvenile offenders' lives.

Criminological theory which explains crime and crime rates has essentially evolved from the urban setting. Its only use to rural areas is that it explains why crime does not occur--the more urban the area, the more crime that occurs. Warner notes that rural areas are distinctly different from urban areas; there tends to be an absence of a criminal/delinquent subculture in rural areas, and offenses are of an individual type rather than group type.

Pawlak, in comparing differences between urban and rural juvenile court practices, found certain factors to be consistent among rural jurisdictions. First, rural courts process more first offenders than urban courts, which deal more with recidivists. This seems largely due to the fact that rural areas have less diversion resources, and as a result, the court is looked upon as a primary agent of intervention. Second, types of crimes varied from rural to urban, with rural areas having more property crimes; on the other hand, urban areas reported more crimes against persons. Third, rural courts use formal hearings more often than urban courts; however, urban courts utilize diagnostic services more often--this again illustrates the greater availability of resources. Lastly, Pawlak found no significant differences between rural and urban courts in their use of institutional commitments other than the fact that rural areas reported both highest and lowest rates for commitments. Two basic explanations were offered: (1) that rural areas try to keep children from being committed since they were known to the community; and (2) since there was a lack of resources, institutional commitments are sometimes used more heavily.

Johnson, in his article on "Crime, Delinquency, and Criminal Justice in Rural America," offers several suggestions to deal with problems of rural programming for juvenile offenders. First, rather than develop an elaborate system of detention facilities, which tend to be over-utilized, consideration ought to be given to developing regional facilities, shelter homes and temporary foster homes. Second, in keeping with the emphasis to reduce the use of detention facilities, general efforts should be toward deinstitutionalization and development of community alternatives, which are affordable to small communities such as group homes, and of preventative programs which emphasize in-home intervention, rather than alternative placements.

CHAPTER I

ISSUES IN RURAL JUVENILE JUSTICE

by Joseph DeJames

It certainly was no coincidence that the first juvenile court, established in Chicago in 1899, was developed in a large city rather than a rural county in Tennessee or Montana. At the turn of the century, delinquency was synonymous with urban poverty, the squalor of slum life and the massive waves of East European immigrants to the cities. Rural areas, on the other hand, were viewed as panaceas for delinquency, and it was thought by reformers that delinquents would be best treated "if they were removed from their homes and placed in a more healthful countryside, preferably in a western state, where they would be exposed to the virtues of middle-class life: sobriety, thrift, industry, prudence and piety."[1]

Since then, delinquency has been thought of as an urban phenomenon, and as a result, most criminological theory has been developed in urban areas. In the 1920's and early 1930's, delinquency studies were an important part of the "Chicago School" of developing urban sociology. Beginning in the 1950's sociologists studied elements of "delinquent subcultures" and "juvenile gangs" to find causes of delinquency. Because of the traditionally close association between urbanism and delinquency, urban models have been developed for delinquency prevention and juvenile justice processing of juvenile offenders through law enforcement, judicial and correctional agencies. National juvenile justice standards, developed by groups such as the Institute of Judicial Administration/American Bar Association (IJA/ABA) and the National Advisory Committee on Criminal Justice Standards and Goals, also have an "urban flavor" to them.

Clearly, the incidence of juvenile crime is lower in rural areas, and the offenses committed by delinquents from rural areas are not as serious as those in urban areas. Nevertheless, rural delinquency is becoming an increasingly important issue with delinquency rates increasing at a faster rate in rural than urban areas. The recent development of several rural juvenile justice programs is also the result of the federal Juvenile Justice and Delinquency Prevention (JJDP) Act of 1974. Rural states, counties and local communities are now receiving federal funds for such programs. The processing of juvenile offenders through rural juvenile justice agencies and the development of rural intervention strategies must reflect the unique characteristics of the rural environment. Accordingly, this chapter analyzes some of the issues faced by rural juvenile justice agencies in handling juvenile offenders.

Urban-Rural Differentials

Although there is broad general consensus that the term "rural" refers

---

[1] J. Lawrence Schultz, "The Cycle of Juvenile Court History," Crime and Delinquency (1973), pp. 457-476.

to populations living in areas of low density and small towns, there are wide variations in the distinctions between "rural," "urban" and "suburban." Depending on one's definition of the imprecise terms "rural" and "nonmetropolitan," 31 to 42 percent of Americans (62 to 82 million persons) live in these areas, which constitute 89 percent of the total area of the United States.

[Note: The Census Bureau defines "rural" as a place with a population under 2,500. Other federal agencies define "rural" as "nonmetropolitan," referring to an area outside a Standard Metropolitan Statistical Area (SMSA)--an area whose central city has a population of at least 50,000.]

Since the basic unit of juvenile justice administration is the county, it should also be noted that of the country's 3,099 counties, 2,463 are outside Standard Metropolitan Statistical Areas.[2] Rural areas are diverse rather than homogeneous in nature and may include farming communities, resort areas, lumber or mining towns, small factory towns and satellites of larger metropolitan centers. The twentieth century migration from rural to urban areas has been reversed since 1970, and nonmetropolitan areas are now growing at a more rapid rate than metropolitan ones. During the period 1970-73, nonmetropolitan areas increased by 4.2 percent; metropolitan areas grew by only 2.9 percent.[3]

What are the characteristics of rural America that influence juvenile justice processing and the development (or lack) of programs? Obviously, major characteristics which differentiate rural from urban areas are low population and geographic isolation. These are strongly related to another characteristic of rural areas which significantly impacts on juvenile justice--a lack of resources such as social services, health care, public transportation and alternative schools. This lack of resources, however, also stems from the reality of rural America being a poor and depressed economic area with a meager tax base and little financial support for such services.

Schultz notes many rural families "cling tenaciously to such early American values as extreme self-reliance, traditionalism, familism, fundamentalism, and fatalism."[4] A traditional conservative ideology, a distrust of state and federal government, and a lack of anonymity also differentiate rural from urban communities. Such values and attitudes color a family's and community's perception of juvenile offenders and the juvenile justice system and must be accounted for when developing programs. However, while some urban-rural differences are clear, others are gradually disappearing. The interchange of people between rural and urban areas through large-scale migration, the influence of urban-centered mass media, greater interdependence of rural and urban economics, and improved transportation are all gradually changing urban-rural differences.

---

[2]Theodore J. Fetter and E. Keith Stott, Jr., "Rural Courts: Trends and Implications," State Court Journal (1977), pp. 35-39.
[3]Calvin L. Beale, The Revival of Population Growth in Nonmetropolitan America, (Washington, DC: Department of Agriculture, Economic Research Service, Economic Research Division, 1975).
[4]Leroy G. Schultz, "Criminal Justice in Rural America," Social Casework (1970), pp. 151-156.

There still remain, however, substantial differences in crime and delinquency rates between rural and urban areas, because of the direct relationship between urbanization and juvenile delinquency. Although it is not always true urban areas with the largest populations and highest densities have the highest delinquency rates, urban areas tend to have higher rates than do suburban areas, and these areas, in turn, have higher rates than do rural areas. Table 1 shows the arrest rates for persons under 18 for cities, suburbs and rural areas in the United States for 1978. The table, using data from the 1972 FBI Uniform Crime Reports, notes the rate of arrests in cities is slightly higher than in suburban areas, yet is almost three times the rural arrest rate for persons under 18. Many explanations exist to explain why there is less crime in rural areas: stable populations, more closely knit families, greater church and school controls and people who are less alienated from their communities than their city counterparts. From a criminal justice perspective, there is less opportunity for certain kinds of crime in rural areas, less accurate records kept by rural law enforcement agencies and fewer persons apprehended for crimes committed.

TABLE 1

Arrest Rates for Persons Under 18 in
Cities, Suburban and Rural Areas - United States
1972 and 1978

Area	Arrest Rates Per 100,000 Population		
	1972	1978	Percent Change
City	1,322	1,254	- 5.1
Suburban	1,069	1,132	+ 5.9
Rural	380	441	+16.1

Source: FBI, Uniform Crime Reports, 1972: 135, 144, 152; and 1978: 202, 211, 220.

Table 1 also shows the change in arrest rates for cities, suburbs and rural areas from 1972 to 1978. The arrest rate for cities decreased slightly, 5.1 percent, while the arrest rate for suburban areas increased slightly, 5.9 percent. However, the arrest rate for persons under 18 in rural areas increased significantly to 16.1 percent. Part of this increase may be related to older juveniles from urban and suburban areas committing offenses in rural communities. Phillips notes that of all persons apprehended by sheriff departments in sampled rural areas in Ohio, 60 percent were urban residents.[5] Obviously, this factor must be taken into account in any program planning effort.

Table 2 (on the following page) analyzes differentials among urban, suburban and rural areas arrest rates of persons under 18 by offense type. In cities, the arrest rates for specific offenses are generally between two and four times higher than comparable rates in rural areas. The only offenses with comparable rates among cities, suburbs and rural areas are "driving under the influence" and "drunkenness." Generally, most juvenile crime in rural areas is of a different character than urban areas. Crimes against persons are mainly an urban phenomenon. Most juvenile offenses in rural areas are minor property offenses. Phillips, in a victimization survey of rural Ohio residents, notes that vandalism is the leading crime in rural Ohio (38 percent of all crimes committed in rural areas) and that vandalism of mailboxes is the property most affected.[6] The same survey noted that larceny was the second leading crime in rural areas.

Characteristics of rural areas such as low population, lack of resources and relative isolation, help to shape a juvenile justice system which is vastly different from juvenile justice systems in urban areas. The following sections discuss practices and issues in rural juvenile justice.

Police

Partially due to the efforts of the Law Enforcement Assistance Administration (LEAA), various national standard-setting groups and technological advances, police departments have become more professional and efficient over the past decade. The use of computers and sophisticated communications hardware, specialization of job responsibilities, training programs and the development of written policies, guidelines, and procedures, are all relatively commonplace in police departments. However, these advancements in police practices have been largely confined to urban and suburban police jurisdictions since many rural police departments do not have a sufficiently large police force, tax base or serious crime problem to warrant such "frills."

Three law enforcement jurisdictions are generally responsible for police functions in rural communities--the state police, county sheriff departments and municipal police departments. Sheriff departments play a more significant role in rural rather than in urban law enforcement since many rural police departments are limited to a few police officers. A number of national standard-setting groups have advocated the development of specialized juvenile units in police departments. Groups advocating this position include the Institute of Judicial Administration/American Bar Association (IJA/ABA), the National Advisory Committee on Criminal Justice Standards and Goals, and the International Association of Chiefs of Police (IACP). However, the small size of many rural police departments often precludes any specialization. To deal with juvenile offenders, urban and suburban areas are making more use of social workers in police departments and multi-service Youth Service Bureaus.

---

[5] G. Howard Phillips, Crime in Rural Ohio (Columbus, Ohio: Department of Agricultural Economics and Rural Sociology, Ohio State University, 1975), p. 10.

[6] Ibid., p. 6.

TABLE 2

Arrest Rates Per 100,000 Population for Persons Under 18 for Selected Offenses in Cities, Suburban and Rural Areas United States, 1978

	Area		
Offense Type	City	Suburban	Rural
Homicide	.9	.7	.5
Forcible Rape	2.4	1.7	1.0
Robbery	25.5	19.4	2.8
Aggravated Assault	21.3	20.8	6.3
Burglary	127.7	123.7	64.4
Larceny	267.5	206.8	50.1
Auto Theft	40.3	34.7	20.3
Other Assaults	46.9	39.5	9.3
Stolen Property	20.5	20.3	6.1
Vandalism	71.1	77.5	23.5
Drug Abuse Violations	76.6	76.1	32.5
Driving Under the Influence	12.8	13.7	14.8
Liquor Law Violations	71.3	71.4	42.9
Drunkenness	23.4	19.4	13.9
Disorderly Conduct	77.8	62.2	12.3
Runaways	88.5	85.2	55.5

Source: FBI, Uniform Crime Report, 1978: 202, 211, 220.

Again, even though the use of such services has been advocated by national standard-setting groups, the population base and size of individual police departments in rural areas often do not warrant their development. However, multi-jurisdiction programs could be developed. A police officer or social worker specializing in juvenile matters could be shared among a number of rural jurisdictions.

Police officers in rural areas usually do not specialize in any particular facet of police work. They are generalists, and in the juvenile justice sphere, they often must perform social work functions in addition to their crime-control functions. Since social services and crisis intervention services are more limited in rural areas, rural police officers are often called upon to address these needs. Their urban counterparts are seldom in this situation. Another major difference between urban and rural police departments stems from the character of the community. In many rural communities "everyone knows everyone else." This raises a major issue, not only in police work, but in the administration of rural justice. The issue is assessing the problems and benefits associated with a police officer's close familiarity with juveniles and their families. On one hand, it can mean greater personal attention to each case, informal resolution of the problem and working with the family and school to prevent future delinquency. In this context, it would mean many status offenders and minor delinquent offenders would be dealt with informally by nonintervention or mediation by the police officer, or by informal referral to a helping agency in the community. On the other hand, increased personal acquaintance in a rural community can lead to favoritism and unequal treatment, especially for juveniles who come from families perceived by the community to be "bad," or for out-of-town juveniles. Thus, there may be more discretion on the part of rural police officers.

Since police policy is often an expression of community standards, the maintenance of "law and order" is an important issue in traditionally conservative rural communities. Since rural police are not confronted with many violent offenses, the standard for a "serious" offense changes when one moves from an urban to a rural community. Vandalism is generally thought to be a minor offense in urban areas, since police by necessity must spend a higher proportion of their time dealing with FBI index offenses--homicide, rape, robbery, aggravated assault, burglary, larceny and auto theft. In a rural area, however, vandalism takes on a different character and the community may demand a "crackdown" on vandals. In practice, this means juveniles may be arrested in rural areas for offenses which in urban areas would result in a reprimand and notification of the parents. This also means that in the name of "law and order" juveniles may be placed in the county jail for relatively minor offenses.

Detention and Jailing of Youth

Perhaps the most significant problem facing rural juvenile justice administration is the routine jailing of youth in rural municipal lockups and county jails. It is estimated that during the mid-1970's approximately 120,000 juveniles per year were held in adult jails, and ten states, most of them rural--Idaho, Ilinois, Kentucky, Minnesota, New Mexico, Ohio, Oregon, Texas, Virginia and Wisconsin--accounted for over 50 percent of the jail admissions. Further, reliance on adult jails for detaining juvenile offenders during the mid-1970's was greatest in the western United States.[7]

---

[7]Community Research Forum, Removing Children from Adult Jails: A Guide to Action (Champaign, Illinois, University of Illinois, 1980), p. 5.

Although dependent or neglected children, status offenders and delinquent youth have been housed in jails for decades, recognition of this as a national problem has been most pronounced in the 1970's, fueled partly by the passage of the federal Juvenile Justice and Delinquency Prevention Act of 1974. Rural states and counties are having the most difficulty in complying with the two most significant provisions of the Act:

> Juveniles who are charged with or who have committed offenses that would not be criminal if committed by an adult, or such nonoffenders as dependent or neglected children, shall not be placed in juvenile detention or correctional facilities.
>
> Juveniles alleged or found to be delinquent and status and nonoffenders shall not be detained or confined in any institution in which they have regular contact with adult persons incarcerated because they have been convicted of a crime or are awaiting trial on criminal charges.

Many urban jurisdictions had little difficulty complying with the provision requiring separation of adults and juveniles when the JJDP Act was passed in 1974. Higher populations bring with them specialization--county jails for adults, juvenile detention facilities for delinquents and shelter care facilities for dependent or neglected children. Many rural areas, on the other hand, have no such specialization in facilities. Often, the only facility available is the county jail--and, in addition to its use for adult criminals, it is also used for both serious and minor delinquent offenders, status offenders or even for children who have been abused by their parents.

One response by rural areas to the "sight and sound" separation requirement of the federal government has been to isolate juveniles from the adults in the jails, literally placing them in solitary confinement and thereby excluding them from the most basic services. Clearly, this arrangement does not fulfill the spirit of the federal law. In response to the dismal failure in many areas to address adequately the jailing of youth, a number of groups are proposing that no juvenile should be held in an adult jail, regardless of the degree of separation. In 1979, for example, the National Coalition for Jail Reform, made up of such diverse groups as the National Sheriff's Association, the American Correctional Association, the National Association of Counties and the American Civil Liberties Union, adopted the position that no person under 18 should be held in an adult jail.

The total prohibition of the jailing of juveniles would certainly be more difficult to achieve in rural areas because of the lack of alternative facilities or resources, and the often vast distances between population centers. However, rural counties have a number of options aside from building juvenile detention facilities. The first is simply not to detain as many juveniles. The Community Research Forum of the University of Illinois, in providing technical assistance for the federal government, collected data on juveniles detained in adult jails and juvenile detention centers in 187 counties in 10 states, most of them rural, in 1978-79. Approximately 55 percent of the children detained in juvenile detention centers and adult jails in these counties were found to be ineligible for detention according to the detention criteria established by the Advisory Committee to the National Institute for Juvenile Justice and Delinquency Prevention.[8] Focusing solely on children in adult jails, comparable findings were reported by the Children's Defense Fund[9] in a nine-state survey. Only 12 percent of the jailed youth were charged with serious offenses against persons. Of the remaining 88 percent who were jailed for property or minor offenses, 18 percent had been charged with a status offense, and four percent had committed no offense at all.

Since relatively few violent or serious offenses are committed by rural delinquents, it is evident that those placed in detention facilities or jails have committed relatively minor offenses. This is partially explained by local community standards--a nonserious delinquent offense in an urban area may be viewed as a serious offense in a rural area, warranting detention or jail. When New Jersey's 1977 detention rates were analyzed by county, it was found that of the five counties with the highest detention rates, four were among the most rural counties in the State.[10]

> [NOTE: The number of juveniles admitted to the county detention center divided by the number of delinquency complaints filed in court].

Since many detained or jailed juveniles in rural areas pose no threat to the safety of the community, they could simply be released to parents or guardians pending disposition of their cases. Other options available to rural counties for compliance with the federal Act including the following:

> Home Detention: In lieu of placement in secure detention, juveniles in this program remain in their homes and their behavior is monitored on a regular basis, usually every day, by youth workers from the probation office. Use of this program reduces the need for secure detention beds.

> Regional Detention Facilities: Since the population base in many rural counties does not warrant the construction of juvenile detention facilities, regional facilities could be built serving a number of rural counties.

> Emergency Foster Homes: Status offenders and minor delinquent offenders who cannot be returned home could be placed in foster homes in lieu of secure alternatives.

> Shelter Care Facilities: These facilities may be used for dependent or neglected children, status offenders and delinquents. Depending on the area's population base, these facilities could also be regionalized. Because most delinquents do not require secure custody and these facilities serve a wide range of children, rural areas

---

[8] Robert C. Kihm, Prohibiting Secure Juvenile Detention: Assessing the Effectiveness of National Standards Detention Criteria, (Champaign, Illinois: Community Research Forum, University of Illinois, 1980), p. 28.

[9] Children's Defense Fund, Children in Adult Jails (Washington, DC: Children's Defense Fund, 1976), pp. 3-4.

[10] Dale Dannefer and Joseph DeJames, Juvenile Justice in New Jersey: An Assessment of the New Juvenile Code, (Trenton, New Jersey: Department of Human Services, 1979), p. 63.

would be better served by the development of nonrestrictive shelter care facilities than secure alternatives.

Juvenile Court

As noted earlier, both the incidence and character of juvenile crime is different in rural America than in urban areas: juvenile arrest rates for virtually every offense type are much higher in urban and suburban areas than in rural areas. This, combined with low population, means that some rural juvenile courts may only hear one or two hundred cases a year, whereas urban courts may hear several thousand juvenile cases each year. Certainly, the number and types of crimes committed by juveniles affects the needs and available resources of the juvenile court. "Although all rural courts are not the same, many have common characteristics including part-time personnel, small, often inadequately trained staffs; shortage of court-related services, lack of specialization of judges, informality of procedures, isolation from professional colleagues; inadequate court facilities and more personal familiarity among criminal justice personnel and with litigants before the court."[11]

It is interesting that many of today's "reforms" in the juvenile justice system such as nonintervention, restitution and dispute settlement have been time-honored practices in rural America. In many rural areas, a frontier ethic of justice which dictates a reluctance to resort to legal solutions, still prevails. For example, in a system where "everyone knows everyone else," there may be a general reluctance to file a complaint against a neighbor's son for a nonserious delinquent offense, when restitution, worked out among the parties, may be all that's needed. However, when a case is forwarded to court, there is a higher likelihood the juvenile will receive more individualized treatment and increased personal contact than in urban areas, due, in part, to the smaller volume of cases, informality of proceedings, and sometimes, prior knowledge of the juvenile's history. In many rural areas, judges may be familiar with the juveniles and their families through social contacts, school or church. As noted earlier, in the context of police, there are both positive and negative elements to this situation. However, this familiarity may be decreasing due to increased migration between urban and rural areas and the increasing number of juvenile offenders from outside the community.

In many states, more juvenile cases are heard by nonlawyer referees, masters or commissioners who have been appointed to serve as judicial hearing officers, than by judges. In fact, many of the judges themselves are not lawyers, and relatively few handle juvenile cases exclusively. Some juvenile court judges are part-time; others are responsible for a multi-county area and are required to "ride the circuit." A number of rural courts are two-person departments--one judge and one probation officer. From a rural judicial perspective, there is lack of specialization in juvenile matters and often, a lack of training in such matters. The adequacy of defense counsel is also questionable in rural areas. There are very few public defender systems in rural areas; rather, the courts must rely on a system of assigned counsel

---

[11]E. Keith Stott, Jr., Theodore J. Fetter, and Laura L. Crites, Rural Courts: The Effect of Space and Distance on the Administration of Justice, (Denver, Colorado: National Center for State Courts, 1977), p. 4.

when a juvenile needs legal counsel. Assigned attorneys receive relatively low pay, usually are not well trained in juvenile matters and often are not well prepared to present an adequate defense.

As in the case with police, a number of national standard-setting groups have recommended a variety of specialized juvenile court related services, including diagnostic and counseling services, juvenile court intake services, diversion programs and specialized probation services. Although the volume of juvenile cases often does not warrant the development of formal programs, such services sometimes exist in another context. Although the court may not have at its disposal a juvenile offender counseling program, a generic youth counseling program may be available in the child welfare sector.

Social Services and Corrections

Since relatively few court-related specialized juvenile services exist in rural areas, there is a higher likelihood that such services would be provided through the child welfare or mental health system. In regard to dispositional alternatives, most national standards advocate a wide range of residential and nonresidential programs, including treatment facilities and secure institutions. Also advocated are the least restrictive alternative as a disposition and community-based alternatives to secure facilities.

Certainly, rural areas do not have the population to warrant such a wide array of services. However, in terms of program development, resources already in existence in the community should be utilized as much as possible, recognizing the alternatives will not always be specialized or for "problem" children. In many areas the church is an important part of rural culture and could be tapped for such services as counseling, volunteers and emergency foster homes. In this regard, contact could also be made with various rural civic organizations. Volunteerism may be an untapped resource in rural areas, specially considering rural residents take great pride in their communities. The use of volunteers could develop an increased awareness on the part of the citizens for the youth needs of the community, in addition to providing a strong link between the community, the child and the juvenile justice system.

When agencies or programs for youth are developed in rural areas, the services could be extended to both juvenile offenders and "trouble-free" youth. Normalization and lack of stigma are inherent in program models of this type and such services also have a higher likelihood of receiving both political and financial support. A multi-services agency could provide counseling and crisis intervention services, recreation services, alternative education and some job training.

When specialized juvenile justice services--such as counseling programs, day treatment, or group homes--are warranted, it may be important to develop such services on a multi-county or community basis. Such arrangements would increase the likelihood of receiving federal funds or make the costs less prohibitive to each of the respective counties or municipalities.

A major issue in rural juvenile justice is the relationship between the availability of resources and services, and commitment to a training school.

Rural judges may often feel that a noncorrectional program or residential alternative is appropriate for a particular juvenile, but their nonavailability increases the likelihood the judge will commit the juvenile to a state correctional institution. Delinquents from rural areas are vulnerable to training school commitments for another reason. As noted earlier, since there is relatively little violent crime in rural areas, the nature of "serious" juvenile crime changes character. For this reason, rural youth may be committed to correctional institutions for offenses which, if committed by juveniles from urban areas, would result in noncorrectional dispositions. As a result, relatively naive rural juveniles may be mixed with aggressive, street-wise juveniles from urban areas. This situation, which raises issues regarding individual treatment and institutional administration, was rasied by Lentz in 1956,[12] and is still an issue today in the administration of rural juvenile justice.

Whatever the reason for training school commitments from rural areas, it is evident rural states place juveniles in correctional institutions at a higher rate than urban states. Data presented in a study by the National Assessment of Juvenile Corrections, University of Michigan[13] shows the following rank order of states with the highest per capita rates of average daily institutional populations in state-run institutions and camps--Wyoming, Nevada, Delaware, Tennessee, New Mexico, Montana, West Virginia, Louisana, Mississippi and Maine. Not only are most of the top ten states rural, but the rates for Wyoming and Nevada are 20 times the rates for Massachusetts and New York, the states with the lowest institutional rates. The nationwide data shows wealthier, more urbanized and industrialized states appear less likely to rely heavily on the use of juvenile institutions and camps. Also, "the greater reliance on these facilities in the less wealthy, more rural and less industrialized states is not due to any greater prevalence of juvenile crimes."[14]

Although community standards are involved in defining a "serious" delinquent offense, rural states must take a close look at the juveniles being committed to state correctional facilities. Many of these juveniles certainly are not "dangerous" by any objective measure, and they certainly would not represent a "threat to the community." For some juveniles, a disposition involving restitution or community service may be more appropriate than a training school commitment. For juveniles requiring out-of-home placement, group homes, residential placements or small regionalized community-based correctional facilities should be utilized as much as possible.

Summary

It is evident rural delinquency is on the rise, but property offenses, mainly vandalism, constitute the rural juvenile delinquency problem. Certainly, the geographic isolation and low population of rural areas means the juvenile justice system is much different than in urban or suburban areas.

---

[12]William P. Lentz, "Rural Urban Differentials and Juvenile Delinquency," Journal of Criminal Law, Criminology and Police Science (47), pp. 331-339.
[13]Robert D. Vinter, George Downs, and John Hall, Juvenile Corrections in the States: Residential Programs and Deinstitutionalization, National Assessment of Juvenile Corrections (Ann Arbor: University of Michigan, 1976), p. 17.
[14]Ibid., p. 18.

Rural areas lack social service resources, specialization and a wide range of juvenile justice programs and facilities--all of which are advocated by a number of national standard-setting groups. However, considering the frequency and seriousness of juvenile crime is much different in rural than urban areas, and that rural areas are vastly different than urban areas in terms of values and attitudes, there is no need to replicate "urban" models to address rural delinquency. It is important to work with the cohesiveness and strengths of rural communities to develop programs and strategies which are relevant to rural areas. Both the police and courts are already involved with nonintervention, diversion and dispute settlement for status offenders and minor delinquent offenders on an informal basis. However, more efforts could be made in this direction. The major problem to be tackled in the administration of rural juvenile justice is the widespread jailing of youth. Many juveniles simply do not need to be detained. Others, including status offenders and minor delinquent offenders, could be held in emergency foster homes. Home detention, regionalized detention and shelter care are other options and alternatives available to rural areas.

It is clear that the rural environment poses challenging issues for the administration of juvenile justice and the efforts to improve rural juvenile justice administration must capitalize on positive aspects of the rural environment. With the informality and greater personal contact, the administration of juvenile justice in rural areas has far more potential than in urban areas. In order to bring the potential to fruition, the development of creative "rural" models which tap the inherent strengths of rural communities is needed.

CHAPTER II

RURAL CRIME, RURAL CRIMINALS, RURAL DELINQUENTS: PAST RESEARCH AND FUTURE DIRECTIONS

by John R. Warner, Jr.

Records from English history indicate that the problem of rural crime is nothing new. Rural crime reached crisis proportions in the latter half of the thirteenth century, when "bands of robbers called Drawlatches and Roberdsmen, . . . concealing themselves in the thick undergrowth by the roadside," waged a reign of terror against travelers. So critical was the problem that in 1285 the Statute of Westminster decreed that roads between market towns...

> . . .shall be enlarged so that there be neither dyke, tree nor bush whereby a man may lurk to do hurt, within two hundred foot on the one side and two hundred foot on the other side of the way (Smith, 1933, p. 7).

Nor is the study of rural crime an innovation. Half a century ago, Sorokin, Zimmerman and Galpin (1930) surveyed the literature on rural crime in 15 countries including the U.S.A., Great Britain, Australia, British India and 11 European nations. Their survey, covering literature between the years 1857 and 1920, led the authors to set forth the following nine propositions:

1. In proportion to the population, the number of crimes or offenses is greater in the cities than in the country.

2. Data concerning the residence of offenders show that the city population yields a greater number of offenders than the country population.

3. Data concerning the place of birth of offenders indicates that cities produce a greater proportion of offenders than rural areas, but this factor is of less importance than residence of the person at the time under consideration.

4. The agricultural population is one of the least criminal of all occupation classes.

5. On the whole the country population is more law-abiding than that of the city.

6. The professional and official classes of the city are definitely less criminal than the agricultural class taken as a whole. This means that the urban population again shows a greater variation than the rural population.

7. In the majority of countries the criminality of the agricultural class is manifested somewhat more strongly in crimes against persons, particularly in homicide, infanticide, and grave assaults, than in crimes against property, with the exception of arson and cattle-stealing, which are predominantly rural crimes. . . . This conclusion must not be interpreted to mean

that the rural or agricultural population generally has a higher rate of crimes against persons than the city population. On the contrary, in many countries the rural rate still remains below the urban rate. But in proportion to all crimes, crimes against persons are a larger percentage in rural areas than in urban areas.

8. Crime in the cities has a finished technique requiring strategy, deceit, scheming and lying, while rural crimes are more direct, more naive, less deceitful and less strategical.

9. The city population yields a greater number of repeaters than the country population.

The author of this paper has surveyed most of the literature published between 1930 and 1979 in an attempt to determine just what has been said about rural crime in the past half-century (Warner, 1978). The major themes developed in that literature and suggested directions for future research will be discussed in this article.

Definition of Rural Crime

The problem of defining "rural crime" pervades the literature. It was noted 46 years ago in what may have been the first book ever published in America on rural crime. Smith (1933) wrote:

> It is necessary to emphasize the fact that the terms "urban" and "rural" often lack any precise significance. Even when closely defined for a specific purpose, no uniform rule applies, with the result that rural crime statistics occasionally include areas which are of urban character in some of their aspects.

Over the past half century we can report "no progress" in the problem recognized by Smith. Clinard (1942) divided the population of offenders at the Iowa Men's Reformatory into three categories: rural--areas with a population of less than 50; village--areas with a population of 50 to 4,999; and urban--areas with 5,000 or more. Wiers (1939), Lagey (1957), Ferdinand (1964), Han (1971), and Phillips (1975) studied "rural counties," which include rural residents and small towns located in those counties. Boggs (1971) used the term "rural" to include "small town and rural residents," and for Lentz (1956) rural meant "all open country and rural trading centers included within the rural community."

The problem of mixing rural persons and residents of small towns in relation to crime rates is illustrated in Table 1 (on the following page) and discussed below.

Small Towns vs. Rural Areas

Following U.S. Census Bureau definitions, the F.B.I.'s Uniform Crime Reports designates as "urban" all communities with a population of 2,500 or more, and distinguishes six classes of cities based on population. Class VI cities are those which are generally called "small towns." They are communities with populations of 2,500 or 9,999. Table 1 displays the ratio of rural crime rates (per 100,000 population) for 30 offenses compared with crime rates

TABLE 1

Ratio of Rural Crime Rates to Small Town Crime Rates[a]

Crime	Ratio (Per 100,000 population)
Fraud	2.90
Offenses against family and children	2.70
Manslaughter by negligence	2.49
Murder and nonnegligent manslaughter	2.46
Forcible rape	1.72
Embezzlement	1.58
Forgery and counterfeiting	1.29
Arson	1.04
Aggravated assault	1.04
Burglary, breaking and entering	1.01
Robbery	1.00
Auto theft	.85
Driving while intoxicated	.84
Runaway	.82
Narcotics and drug violations	.81
Prostitution and commercialized vice	.80
Possession of stolen property	.74
Other assaults	.72
All other offenses	.72
Other sex offenses	.68
Weapons violations	.63
Drunkenness	.59
Vagrancy	.56
Suspicion	.46
Larceny	.44
Gambling	.43
Vandalism	.40
Liquor violations	.39
Disorderly conduct	.29
Curfew violations	.12

[a]From United States Department of Justice, Federal Bureau of Investigation, Uniform Crime Reports 1976 (Washington, D.C.: GPO, 1977). Based on arrests per 100,000 population.

for small towns. As demonstrated in the Table, rural crime is a different sort of thing than small town crime. In 1976 there were 10 categories of crime for which police made arrests more often in rural areas than in small towns, and 19 categories for which police made more arrests in small towns. Fraud, offenses against family and children, manslaughter and murder occurred more than twice as often in rural areas as in small towns, and rape and embezzlement were reported more than one and one-half times as often in rural areas as in small towns. On the other end of the scale, there were seven categories of crime which were reported more than twice as often in small towns as in rural areas. Small towns and rural areas are not homogenous areas!

Accuracy of Official Records

The inaccuracy of police records is thoroughly documented and discussed in all criminology textbooks. The problem is probably greater in rural areas than in cities and this problem has led some (Schlutz, 1976) to doubt that urban-rural differences are as great as they seem. The problem was noted by Smith (1933) long ago, when he reported:

> . . . the tendency of rural residents to withhold information concerning offenses from police officials and the defective records of rural officials undoubtedly affect these comparisons.

Magnitude

It has long been recognized that crime rates are higher in urban areas than in rural areas, and that for most (but not all) crimes there is a positive correlation between the population size and crime rates. Polk (1967) writes:

> Over time, one of the most consistent regularities found in crime statistics is the higher overall rate of crime in urban as compared to rural areas. However, the degree to which urban rates exceed rural rates varies with offense, with locale and with time.

The point is illustrated in Table 2 (on the following page) from Uniform Crime Reports (1976) data for arrest rates in six classes of cities and in rural areas.

Rural Crimes

Sorokin et al. found that the crimes of arson, cattle-stealing, infanticide and specific violations of agricultural laws were more often committed in rural areas than in urban areas, and he found that crimes against the person were more common in rural areas (in comparison to all crimes in rural areas) than property crimes.

In order to determine what crimes are "officially" rural crimes, we divided the arrest rates for 30 categories of crimes in rural areas by the arrest for those categories in urban areas, using data from Uniform Crime Reports (1976). The results are listed in Table 3 (on page 21) for the 13 "rural crimes."

TABLE 2

Arrest Rates for Cities and Rural Areas

Area type	Rate of arrests per 100,000 population
Class I Cities 52 cities over 250,000	1,494
Class II Cities 98 cities 100,000 to 250,000	1,333
Class III Cities 235 cities 50,000 to 100,000	1,139
Class IV Cities 564 cities 25,000 to 50,000	1,089
Class V Cities 1402 cities 2,500 to 10,000	930
Class VI Cities 5264 cities 2,500 to 10,000	778
Rural Areas 1,904 areas reporting	537

Source: Uniform Crime Reports, 1976. Index crimes only.

According to F.B.I. information, the four crimes which are reported more often in rural areas than in urban areas are offenses against family and children, fraud, manslaughter by negligence and driving while intoxicated. Of these, manslaughter is certainly explained by traffic deaths on the highways and by hunting accidents, neither of which seem to be characteristic of rural people but only of the rural location.

It is interesting to note that Sorokin et al. (1930) list fraud, forgery and intemperance (alcohol) as particularly urban crimes, while all three appear very high on the rural end of the continuum according to the Uniform Crime Reports information.

TABLE 3

Ratio of Rural Arrest Rates to City Rates[a]

Crime	Ratio
Offenses against family and children	2.45
Fraud	2.09
Manslaughter by negligence	2.08
Driving while intoxicated	1.21
Murder and nonnegligent manslaughter	.98
Forgery and counterfeiting	.97
Arson	.82
Aggravated assault	.79
Liquor violations	.78
Forcible rape	.77
Runaways	.71
Narcotics	.70
Burglary and breaking and entering	.70

[a]From Uniform Crime Reports 1976. Ratio obtained by dividing rural crime rate (arrests per 100,000 population) by urban rate. The total rural/urban ratio was .63. The 13 crimes listed here are those for which the ratio is higher than .63.

Lentz (1956) compared rural and urban boys in the Wisconsin School for Boys. He found that rural boys were more often charged with sex offenses, nominal breaking and entering, truancy and general misconduct, while urban boys were more often charged with serious breaking and entering, serious and nominal theft and car theft. Rural sex offenses tended to be indecent exposure, rape of small girls and sodomy, while urban boys were more often involved in prostitution and "gang shags."

In his study of delinquency in rural Michigan, Wiers (1939) found that burglary and stealing constituted 60 percent of the offenses for which male delinquents were charged, while thirty percent of the females were charged as being "ungovernable," and 19 percent were charged with sex offenses.

Phillips (1975) found that in rural Ohio vandalism was the most common crime and that rural mail boxes were the primary targets of this vandalism. Ranking second was theft and the primary targets of rural theft were gasoline tanks in farm yards. Rural sheriffs reported, however, that 60 percent of their arrests were of urban boys.

Gibbons (1972) shows that in rural Oregon "folk crimes" are the greatest problem faced by law enforcement officers. Folk crimes include highway violations and violations of hunting and fishing codes. Ferdinand (1964) found that as urbanism increased, offenses against authority increased (status offenses), while offenses against property remained constant for juveniles in Michigan.

Characteristics of Rural Offenders

Although several studies deal with the issue of rural offenders, perhaps the best sketch was developed by Clinard (1942, 1944, 1960) more than three decades ago. According to Clinard, the typical rural offender is characterized by the following.

1. Rural offenders were highly mobile as compared to rural non-offenders.

2. Rural offenders participated only to a limited extent in local community affairs.

3. Rural offenders tended to establish "impersonal" relationships.

4. Their criminal or delinquent behavior commenced relatively late in their youth.

5. They did not generally engage in organized criminal activity.

6. Their criminality was largely adventitious.

7. Their knowledge of criminal techniques was limited.

8. They did not conceive of themselves as criminals or of their acts as crimes.

9. Delinquent gangs were not an important factor in the lives of rural offenders.

Crime Rates as a Variable of Rural Structure or Rural Culture?

Using 10 "structural variables," Quinney (1966) compared crime rates in rural, urban and metropolitan areas. Those "structural variables" were: median years of schooling, median family income, percent white collar males, percent non-white, percent change in residence, percent employed in manufacturing, occupational diversity, percent aged 50 and over, percent females in the labor force, and percent owner-occupied dwelling. He found that rural and urban areas were "more sensitive to structural variations in relation to crime rates than were the larger (metropolitan areas)."

The question of rural structure and rural culture emerges from a visual analysis of Graph 1 (on the following pages). Here crime rates for six classes of cities and for rural areas are presented graphically, superimposed on the national average.

Essentially four patterns emerge. The first pattern fits the popular stereotype of urban-rural crime rates, as illustrated by the graph for robbery. Here the rates are highest in the most urban areas and decrease with the size of the community. There is a simple positive correlation between population and crime rates. This is the most common pattern, characterized by 15 categories of crime including most property crimes, vice (sex, narcotics, gambling), arson (contrary to Sorokin's findings), runaways, "other assaults," vagrancy, suspicion and weapons violations. The 15 categories

Graph 1: Crime and Population Areas: 1976

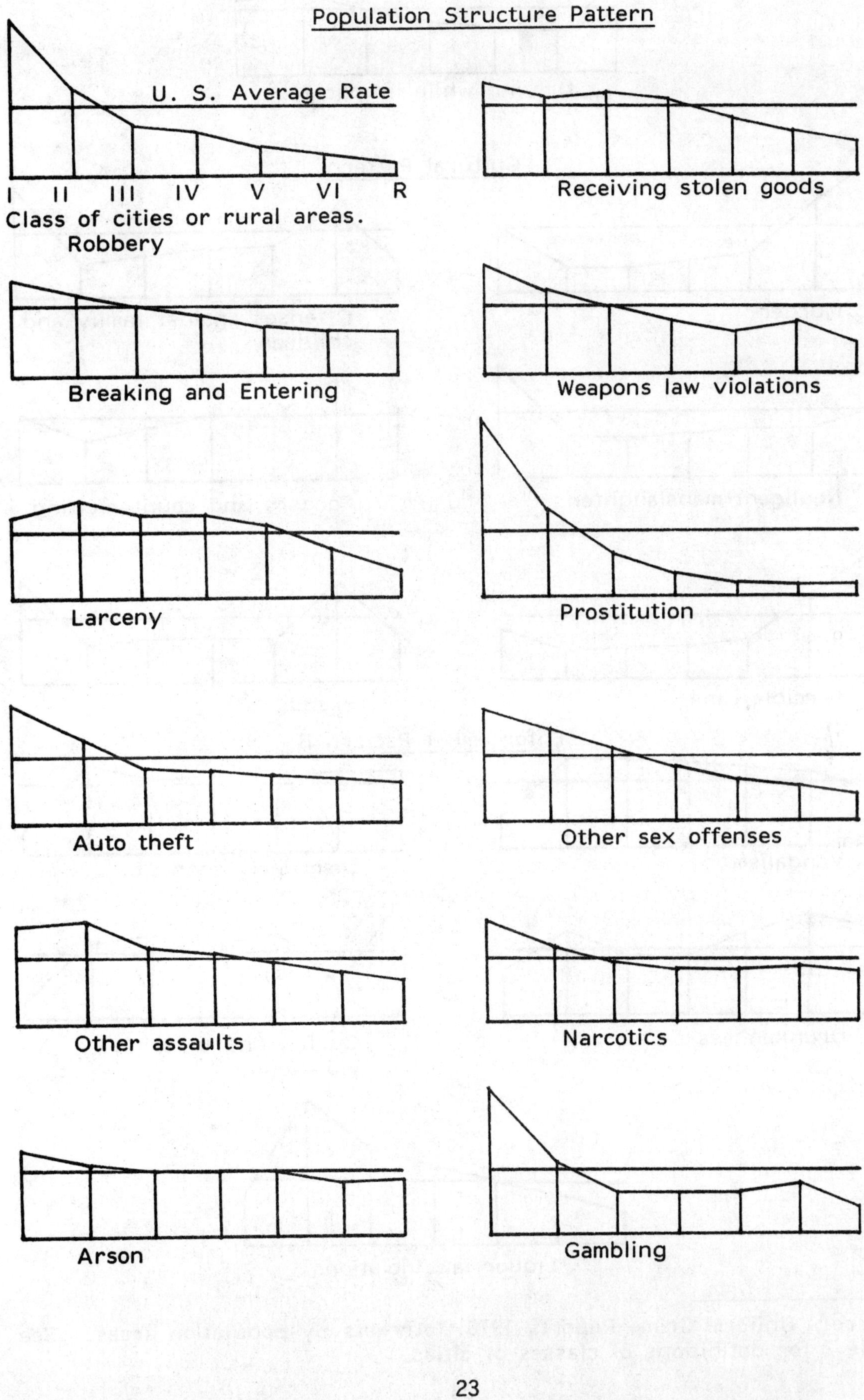

Enforcement Pattern A

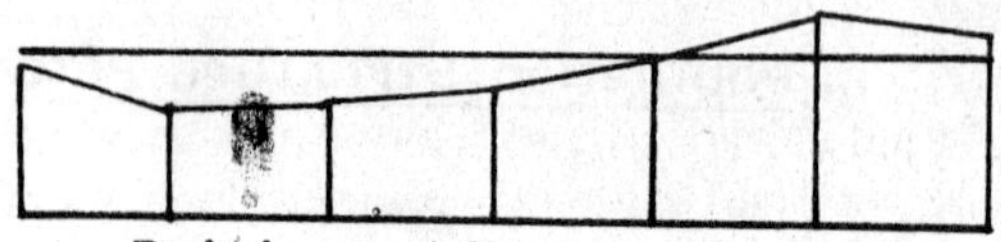

Driving while intoxicated

Cultural Pattern

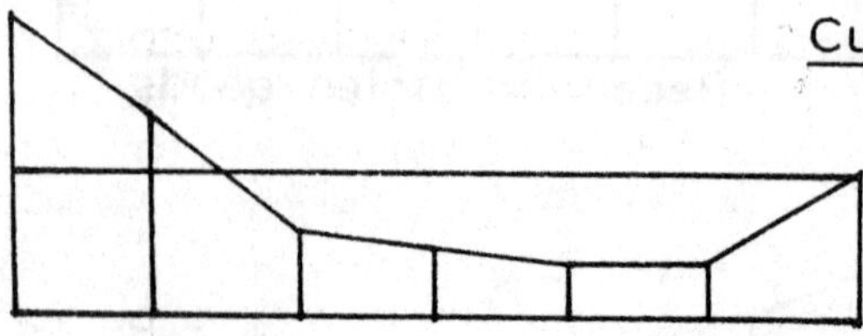

Murder

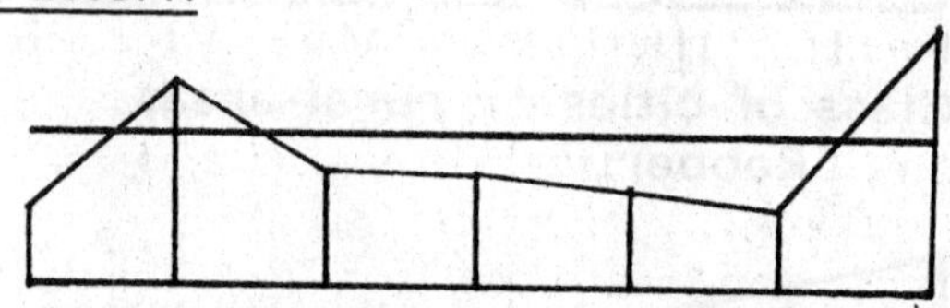

Offenses against family and children

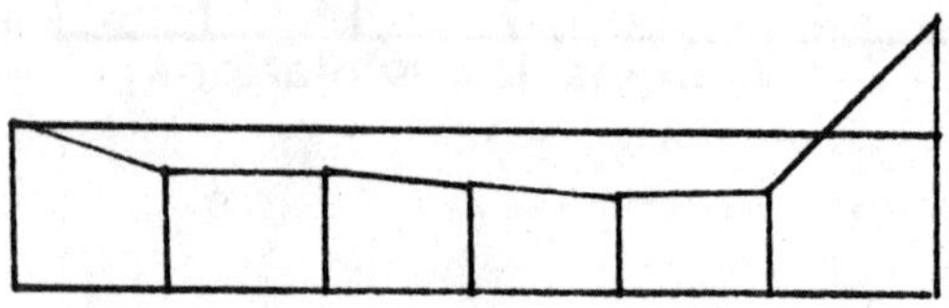

Negligent manslaughter

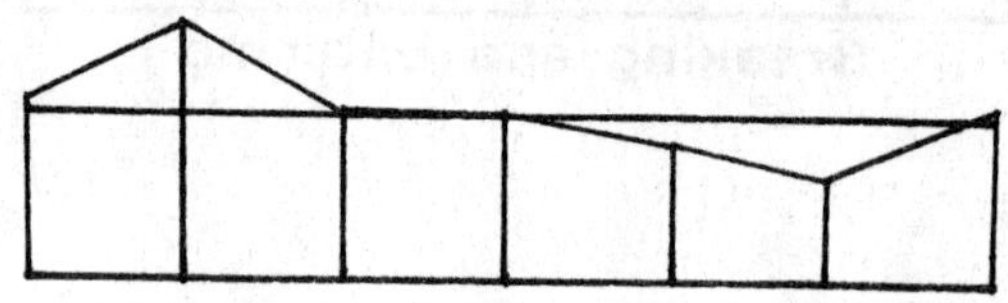

Forgery and counterfeiting

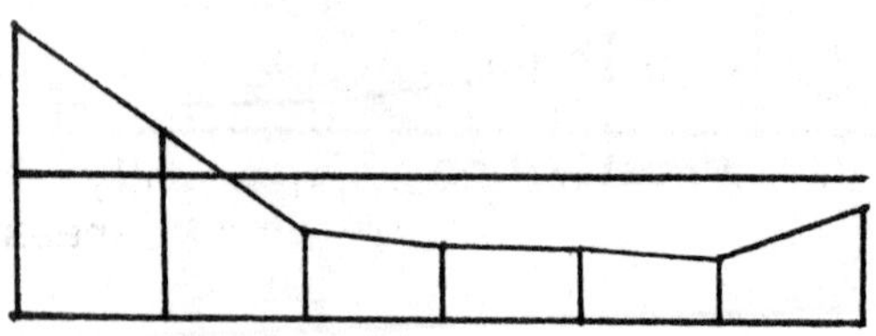

Forcible rape

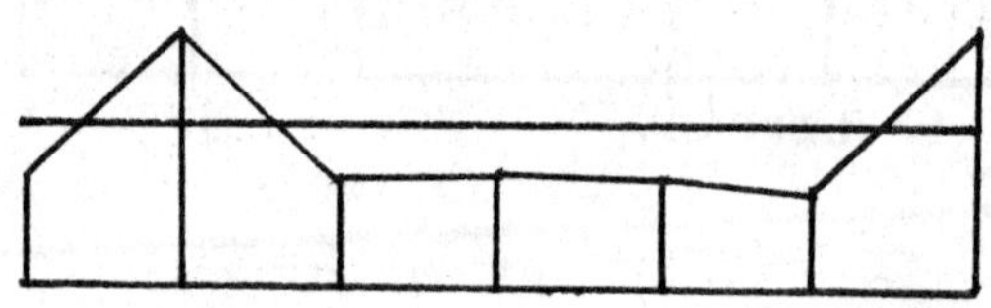

Fraud

Enforcement Pattern B

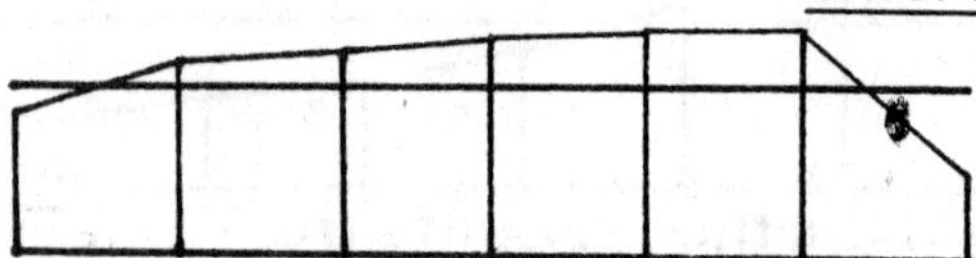

Vandalism

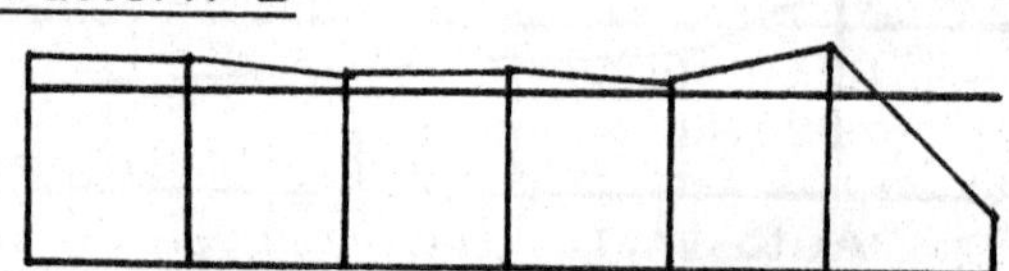

Disorderly conduct

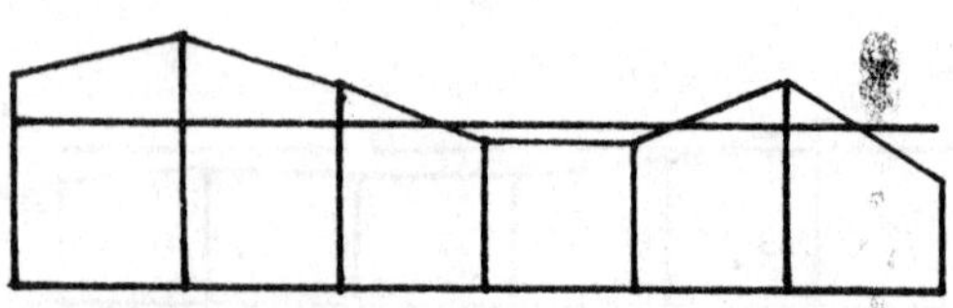

Drunkenness

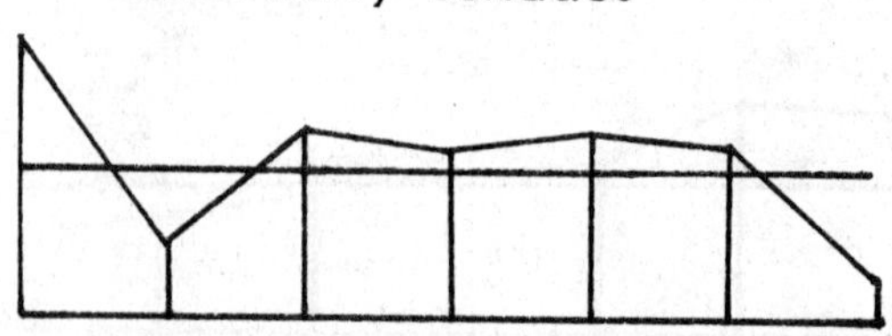

Curfew and loitering violations

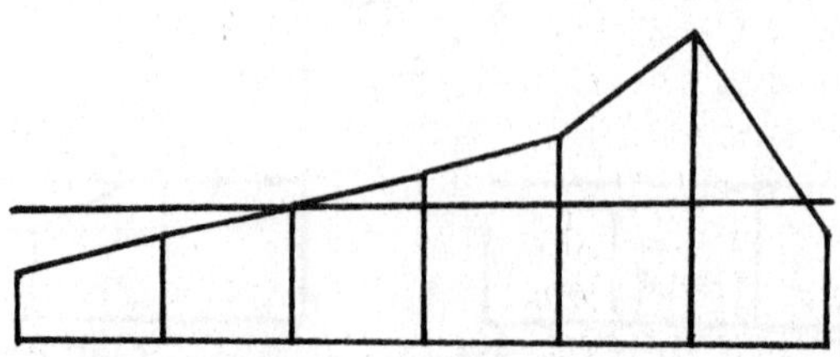

Liquor law violations

Source: Uniform Crime Reports 1976. Arrests by population areas. See Table 2 for definitions of classes of cities.

illustrate, I believe, a structural pattern in which crime rates are a function of population density.

The second pattern indicates a negative correlation between crime rates and population density: as population decreases, crime rates increase. This pattern is illustrated by one category only, driving while intoxicated. This arrest pattern might well be a function of police boredom rather than population structure! Studies by Wiers (1939), Lentz (1956), Polk (1967), and Gibbons (1972) suggest that rural justice is more punitive than urban justice. Persons in similar cities and rural areas are often arrested for minor crimes which would be overlooked in more urban areas and judges or juries are more punitive in smaller cities and rural areas than in larger cities. Lacking the excitement of urban crime, police in rural areas "over-arrest" violators of minor ordinances, such as traffic laws. I suggest labeling the pattern Enforcement Pattern A.

The third pattern is characterized by a radical discontinuity between rural crime rates and the structural pattern for cities. The pattern is illustrated by categories of murder, manslaughter, forcible rape, forgery and counterfeiting, fraud and offenses against family and children. In each category there is a negative correlation between population and crime rates for cities, yet crime rates increase in rural areas. I suggest labeling this pattern a cultural pattern. This is suggested as an untested hypothesis. Because population structure does not account for these crime rates in rural areas, the explanation may lie in cultural characteristics of rural society.

The fourth pattern is the reverse. Here crime rates generally increase or remain stable as population decreases for cities, yet for rural areas crime rates decrease. This pattern is illustrated by vandalism, drunkenness, liquor law violations, disorderly conduct, curfew and loitering violations. In attempting to make sense out of this pattern, I am particularly mindful of the Phillips study (1975) indicating that vandalism was the farmer's number one complaint. I suggest that the low arrest rate for these crime categories in rural areas is most likely a function of the difficulties of rural law enforcement rather than of rural structure or rural culture. I label this Enforcement Pattern B, but lacking better information I recognize that this is done only as an hypothesis.

Type of Rural Community

Crime rates vary with the economic characteristics of rural areas, as noted by Yoke (1932), Wiers (1939) and by Polk (1967). Polk writes:

> From time to time and place to place, there have been exceptions to this trend (low crime rates in rural areas). Elliott (1944) suggests that the existence of "frontier mores accounted for high rates of crime in some communities even though small in size during the developing years of the United States, and may still have an impact. Thus, frontier towns, river towns, seaports, and border areas have had high rates of crime regardless of the degree of population concentration. Logging counties and mining counties have also been found to have relatively high crime rates, in spite of the nonurban classification of the counties. This has often been accounted for by the preponderance in these areas of young, single males who constitute a high criminal risk category.

Wiers found that among rural counties in Michigan delinquency rates were lowest for agricultural counties, followed by upstate logging and mining counties and higher still for rural industrial counties. Yoke found that crime rates were higher in rural coal producing counties in West Virginia than in rural counties with higher agricultural populations.

Ecological Studies

Using a method not unlike the Shaw (1929) concentric circle studies of crime rates in Chicago, Smith (1937) studied delinquency rates in "concentric" tiers of counties surrounding urban areas in Kansas.[1] Results were similar to those in Chicago's concentric zones. Delinquency rates were highest for the urban counties, followed by the next tier of counties adjacent to the urban county, and were lower still for the second tier, etc.

Lagey (1957) plotted the location of residence of delinquents in a rural county in Western Pennsylvania over a three-year period in the 1950's. He discovered that there was not a random scattering of dwelling places of delinquents, but that indeed they seemed to be located primarily in four very specific areas of the county. Furthermore, there was a tendency for delinquents to live within 500 feet of a railroad track or a river, creating a "ribboning" pattern. Below is Lagey's county map plotting the homes of juvenile delinquents.

A Regional Analysis of Crime Rates

A larger ecological approach to crime is the regional analysis developed by Lottier (1938) and sustained by Shannon (1954) and Kowalski (1979).

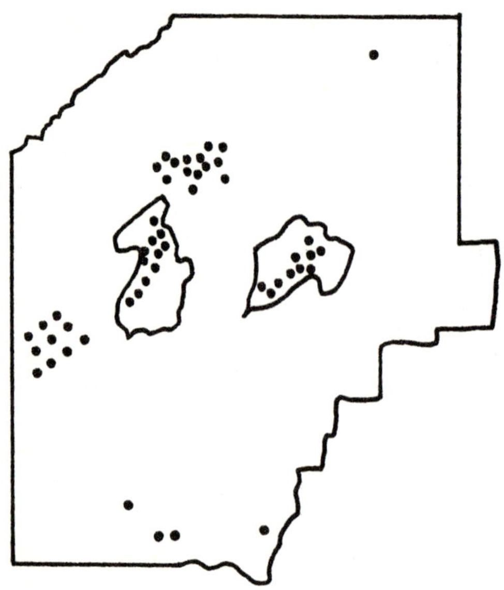

Residences of juvenile delinquents in Venango County, Pa., 1954-56. From Lagey (1957, p. 232).

---

[1]Smith does not refer to the work of Shaw, but to Park (1929).

Lottier utilized the (then) newly developed Uniform Crime Reports to determine crime rates for several categories of crimes in the 48 states. Lottier ranked the states by crime rates for murder, robbery and larceny, developing six rank-groups with eight states in each group. Plotting the rank-groups on the U.S. map revealed clear and definite regional patterns of crime rates. All eight states ranking in the top (highest rate per hundred thousand) rank-group for murder were Southern states, while six of the eight states ranking lowest in homicide rates were the six New England states, and the other two states in that group were northern states--Wisconsin and North Dakota.

For robbery the high-ranking group turned out to be a belt of central states from Kentucky to Colorado, while New England states again ranked lowest. The regional pattern for larceny was also clear: seven of the eight states with highest larceny rates were Western states, from Texas to Oregon, and again New England states ranked lowest.

The pattern has clear implications for the study of rural crime (or urban crime for that matter), particularly in that none of the states ranking highest in murder, robbery and larceny were urban-industrial states.

Patterns of change are seen through similar studies by Shannon (1954) and Kowalski (1979). Kowalski's maps indicate that robbery particularly has shifted to urban states, while the most stable pattern is that of Southern homicide.

The South: A Region of Violence?

Because the South is a rural region, and because the caricature of Southern violence is rural violence, we have included in this essay a discussion of those studies which deal with Southern violence.

> A tendency toward violence has been one of the character traits most frequently attributed to Southerners. In various guises, the image of the violent South confronts the historian at every turn: dueling gentlemen and masters whipping slaves, flatboatmen indulging in a rough-and-tumble fight, lynching mobs, country folk at a bear-baiting or a gander-pulling, romantic adventurers on Caribbean filibusters, brutal police, panic-stricken communities harshly suppressing real and imagined slave revolts, robed night riders engaging in systematic terrorism, unknown assassins, church burners, and other less physical expressions of a South whose mode of action is frequently extreme. The image is so pervasive that it compels the attention of anyone interested in understanding the South (Hackney, 1969).

High homicide rates in the South were observed at least a century ago (Redfield, 1880) and the topic of Southern violence has been the source of numerous scientific essays (not to mention works of fiction). One of the first authors to accumulate quantitative data to support the description of the South as "that part of the United States lying below the Smith and Wesson line" was H.C. Brearley (1934). He found that during the five years from 1920 to 1924 the homicide rate for Southern states was more than two and one-half times greater than for the rest of the nation.

Cash (1941) explains Southern violence by various hypotheses: frontier mentality, cult of honor, life on the plantation, defeat in the Civil War, disrespect for the developing institutions of law after the Civil War because they were administered by "carpetbaggers." Hackney finds most plausible the thesis that it is the relative absence of institutions of law enforcement, the strength of the plantation in maintaining order prior to the Civil War and the disrespect for agencies during Reconstruction which explains Southern violence.

We cannot review the debate over Southern violence, but want only to note that it has been a controversial topic with heated arguments defending and offending Southern culture. [See Porterfield, 1949; Pettigrew, 1962; Gastil, 1971; Loftin and Hill, 1974; and Doerner, 1975.]

Alaska: Crime in the Bush

The heterogeneous character of rural crime becomes clear to the spellbound audiences of John Angell, describing his study of crime in the Alaskan bush country. Pursuing his study on dogsled and Piper Club across an expanse of land and islands as broad as that from Baltimore to Los Angeles, Angell (1978, 1979) describes pre-literate villages terrorized by a drunken clansman, the problems of policing and administering justice when one officer is responsible for literally thousands of square miles of barren land north of the Arctic Circle, where villages of less than 100 inhabitants call for police over shortwave radio, and where a hungry pack of dogs nearly eats a terrified child necessitating a trip to a hospital equal to the distance between Boston and Chicago. No complete study of rural crime can overlook this fascinating description of one more face of a complex issue.

Crime in Developing Countries

Further expanding the kaleidoscopic character of our topic, Clinard and Abbott (1973) bring together "most of the existing findings on crime in Africa, Asia, and Latin America, and the results of our own extensive research in Uganda." The authors observe that almost no standard work on urbanization nor on criminology deals with their topic, while in fact "one measure of the effective development of a country probably is its rising crime rate."

While their focus is on urbanization and change, the process of urbanization is, of course, only possible in less-than-urban areas. This study of crime in developing countries is indeed a study of rural-urban dynamics.

Criminological Theory and Rural Crime

Criminological theory has developed in an urban setting and is, to some extent, an explanation of urban crime. Most theories, whatever the brand, explain why crime rates increase with increased population density. The flip side is a theory which explains why rural areas are relatively crime-free. What is needed is not an explanation of why crime does not happen in rural areas, but a theory which explains why it does happen. With this in mind, we shall survey that criminological research which draws upon theoretical explanations in an interpretation of rural crime.

Absence of a Criminal Subculture in Rural Areas

The rural community is generally free of alternative cultures or subcultures, including criminal subcultures. Thus, a person may deviate from community expectations in rural America and he may find a few friends to join him. But he will not find a value system, a tradition, a social organization, a profession or a jargon which will support him in his deviance.

> In rural areas, there is a comparative absence of continuity in the criminal culture as compared with the interstitial slum areas of a more heterogeneous urban culture (Polk, 1967).

In his study of rural crime and rural criminals in America, Clinard (1942) writes:

> As long as there exists a predominant measure of personal relationship and informal social control in the farm and village areas, it will be impossible for a separate criminal culture to exist. Without the presence of criminal social types, the volume of crime committed by rural residents will continue to be small as compared with that of more urban areas.

Clinard (1960) later confirmed this hypothesis in Sweden as well.

While subculture theory may be used to explain the relatively low property crime rates in rural areas, Kaplan (1961) uses subculture theory to explain the relatively high rate of crimes against persons.

> Differences in rural and urban (crime rates) can perhaps be explained in terms of the differences between urban and rural subcultures. The relative homogeneity of the rural areas and the techniques of social control are probably explanatory of the differences in property crimes. Differences in crimes against the person are similarly explainable, although the relatively greater rate for crimes against the person in rural areas can probably be understood in terms of isolation, self sufficiency, sensitivity to personal affront, and an individualistic tradition.

Differential Association

> Most rural offenders are of the individual rather than of the group type. Their differential association has been of an occasional or fortuitous character (Clinard, 1960).

Gibbons (1972) questions the applicability of Sutherland's theory of differential association to rural crime. In his sketch of "criminals of the hinterland" in rural Oregon, Gibbons (1972) writes:

> Most of the offenders who are the subject of this research are petty lawbreakers. Not many of them resemble professional criminals or other career criminals who acquired antisocial attitudes out of some process of differential association. Instead, it may be that the offenses of many of the individuals in this hinterland area stemmed more from situational contingencies and influences than from criminal motivation.

In his study of rural offenders, Clinard (1944) found that two-thirds of the farm boys had not been associated with groups of boys who stole, and that 87 percent of the boys who committed serious thefts had not been so affiliated. "More often, where differential association occurred, it was with one or two companions rather than with gangs. At times the companions were chance acquaintances whom they met in town," he reported.

Anomie and Rural Crime

Generally the theory of anomie suggests a quality of urban life. Durkheim's (1964) mechanical solidarity is characterized by urban-industrial life. Wirth (1938) describes the anomie of urban life as follows:

> The superficiality, the anonymity, and the transitory character of urban-social relations make intelligible. . .the sophistication and rationality generally ascribed to city-dwellers.

Using Srole's (1956) anomia questions and scale, Killian and Grigg (1962) found little difference between urban and rural residents so far as anomie could be measured. In fact, Lagey (1957) and Clinard (1944) suggest that the presence of anomie in rural areas might indeed explain some rural crime. Lagey finds that rural delinquents are isolated, that "the rural offender may suffer from anomia." In Clinard's (1942) study he found that:

> . . . the impersonality in the lives of the farm and village offenders seemed to be (due to) a lack of general participation in community organization.

Ball and Lilly (1971) compared the anomia (Srole scale) scores of (normal) male students in an "urban" public school in West Virginia, only to discover that these students displayed a higher anomia score than "tough" boys from a high-delinquency area in Columbus, Ohio. A question for further research is this: Do West Virginia boys score high on the anomia scale because they are rural, or because they are Appalachian, or both?

Alienation

Using "perceived limited opportunities" as an indicator of alienation, Han (1971) found a high alienation factor among rural youths in the Upper Cumberland region of Tennessee.

Changing Crime Rates in Rural America

In 1972 the ratio of rural crimes to urban crimes (Uniform Crime Reports 1976) was two to five. By 1976 that ratio had increased to three to five. That great increase in the portion of rural to urban crimes suggests a radical change in the nature of the imaginary peaceful countryside. Whether this 50 percent increase (2,079/100,000 in 1972, 3,171/100,000 in 1976) in rural arrests indicates improved record keeping or increased rural crime, a historic view indicates that this is not the first such relative increase. Smith (1933) points to other "epidemics" of rural crime in other ages. Citing Webb and Webb (1913), Smith writes of rural England:

> For the first half of the eighteenth century, all evidence leads to the impression that crime and disorder were much less prevalent in the rural districts and the provincial towns than in the metropolis . . . After the middle of the century the picture gradually changes for the worse. With the increase in vagrancy, coupled with the growth of passenger traffic and mails, there appears on the great roads, the professional highwayman. [There was also] a general increase in rural delinquency (Smith, 1933, p. 7).

Smith also reports a threefold increase in rural crimes compared to urban crimes in England between 1911 and 1928.

Bloch (1949) is one of the few scholars who has focused on social change as a variable tied to rural crime. Block studied the effects of the Great Depression on rural crime, comparing offenders appearing before the St. Lawrence (New York) County Court in 1927-1929 with those in 1939-1941.

The Administration of Rural Justice

Bruce Smith (1933) has given us an early start in the analysis of rural justice. His historical approach presented under a single cover a discussion of the rural sheriff, the constable and county constabularies, the origins and development of state police, the county coroner and the rural justice of peace. He concludes his work with a chapter entitled "Outlines of Future Development." An interesting study would be a review of this work and an analysis of actual developments from that time to this. But that is for another researcher at another time. [See also Esselstyn, 1953; Boggs, 1971; Poveda, 1972; Schultz, 1976].

Discussion: Directions for Future Research

The above survey has been presented to indicate the major themes--and some of the results--of the studies to date in the emerging field of rural crime. I want to close with suggested directions for further research. The field needs:

1. A better history.

2. Clear separation of "rural" and "small town" areas.

3. Work in both "small town" and "rural areas."

4. Continued work in the analysis of the culture of rural areas which might help explain the etiology of rural violence.

5. Development of crime-category studies: fraud, manslaughter, arson, etc.

6. Studies determining whether it is true that rural police and rural courts are more punitive than urban police and courts, and if so, why.

7. Particular studies of rural violence in the home as suggested by the extremely high rates of rural, as compared to urban, home violence; included should be studies of incest as well as assaultive behavior.

8. Regional studies--Appalachia, Midwestern farm areas; Southern crime, etc.

9. Studies focusing on economic types of rural counties: agricultural, coal mining and other extracting industries, lumber industries, fishing industries, etc.

10. Development of studies which distinguish between rural structure and rural culture as criminogenic variables.

11. Improved self reports, cohort studies and victim reports.

12. Replication and earlier studies.

13. Class and social structure studies: farm workers and farm owners, independent farm owners and corporation farming areas.

14. Racial and ethnic studies of crime in rural areas.

15. Studies over time, including studies of social change, development, urbanization.

16. Studies which evaluate the effects of rapid social change resulting from specific events, such as the energy crisis, war, depression, recessions and inflation.

17. The application of criminological theory: anomie, alienation, differential association, subcultural theories, gangs and isolates, Parsons' pattern variables, Durkheim's "mechanical solidarity," Gemeinschaft, culture lag theory, etc.

18. Inter-institutional studies: rural religion and rural crime, the rural school and rural crime, the rural family, etc.

19. Studies of urban persons in rural areas and particularly the growing influence of organized crime in rural areas.

20. The effects of legislation and court decisions at the state and federal level (Appalachian Act, Juvenile Justice and Delinquency Prevention Act, etc.).

21. Studies of female criminals in rural areas [for a good start, see Steffensmeier and Jordan, 1978, and Ferdinand 1964.]

22. Finally, it will be important to read the existing literature in order to gain a sense of direction (see Warner, 1978).

BIBLIOGRAPHY

Angell, John. Alaska Village Police Training: An Assessment and Recommendations. Anchorage: Criminal Justice Center of the University of Alaska, 1978.

__________. Alaskan Village Justice: An Exploratory Study. Anchorage: Criminal Justice Center of the University of Alaska, 1979.

__________. "Crime in the Bush Country of Alaska." (Paper presented before the Annual Meeting of the Academy of Criminal Justice Sciences), 1979.

Ball, Richard A., and Lilly, J. Robert. "Juvenile Delinquency in an Urban County." Criminology, 9 (1971).

Bloch, Herbert A. "Economic Depression as a Factor in Rural Crime." Journal of Criminal Law and Criminology, 40 (1949).

Boggs, Sarah L. "Formal and Informal Crime Control: An Explanatory Study of Urban, Suburban and Rural Orientations." The Sociological Quarterly, 12 (1971).

Brearley, H.C. "The Pattern of Violence." In W.T. Couch (Ed.), Culture in the South. Chapel Hill: University of North Carolina Press, 1934.

Cash, Wilbur J. The Mind of the South. New York: Alfred A. Knopf, Inc., 1941.

Clinard, Marshall B. "The Process of Urbanization and Criminal Behavior." American Journal of Sociology, 48 (1942).

__________. "Rural Criminal Offenders." American Journal of Sociology, 50 (1944).

__________. "A Cross-cultural Replication of the Relation of Urbanism to Criminal Behavior." American Sociological Review, 25 (1960).

__________. and Donald Abbott. Crime in Developing Countries. New York: John Wiley & Sons, 1973.

Doerner, William G. "A Regional Analysis of Homicide Rates in the United States. Criminology, 13 (1975).

Durkheim, Emile. The Division of Labor in Society. London: The Free Press, 1964.

Elliott, Mable A. Crime and the frontier mores. American Sociological Review, 9 (1944).

Esselstyn, T.C. The Social Role of a County Sheriff. Journal of Criminal Law, Criminology and Police Science, 44 (1953).

Ferdinand, Theodor N. "The Offense Patterns and Family Structures of Urban, Village and Rural Delinquents." Journal of Criminal Law and Criminology, 55 (1964).

Gastil, Raymond D. "Homicide and a Regional Culture of Violence." American Sociological Review, 36 (1971).

Gibbons, Donald C. "Crime in the Hinterland." Criminology, 10 (1972).

Hackney, Sheldon. "Southern Violence." In Hugh Davis and Ted R. Gurr (Eds.), The History of Violence in America. New York: Bantam Books, 1969.

Han, Wan Sang. "Alienation, Deviation-Proneness, and Perception of Two Types of Barriers among Rural Adolescents." Social Forces, 49 (1971).

Kaplan, Sidney J. "The Geography of Crime." In Joseph S. Roucek (Ed.), Sociology of Crime. New York: Philosophical Library, 1961.

Killian, Lewis M. and Grigg, Charles M. "Urbanism, Race, and Anomia." American Journal of Sociology, 67 (1962).

Kowalski, Greg. "The Spatial Distribution of Criminal Offenses by States, 1970-1976." (Paper presented before the Annual Meeting of the Academy of Criminal Justice Sciences), 1979.

Lagey, Joseph C. "The Ecology of Juvenile Delinquency in the Small City and the Rural Hinterland." Rural Sociology, 22 (1957).

Lentz, William P. "Rural-Urban Differentials and Juvenile Delinquency." Journal of Criminal Law, Criminology and Police Science, 47 (1956).

Loftin, Colin and Hill, Robert H. "Regional Subculture and Homicide: An Examination of the Gastil-Hackney Thesis." American Sociological Review, 39 (1974).

Lottier, Stuart. "Distribution of Criminal Offenses in Sectional Regions." Journal of Criminal Law and Criminology, 29 (1938).

Park, Robert E. "Urbanization as Measured by Newspaper Circulation." American Journal of Sociology, 35 (1929).

Pettigrew, Thomas and Spier, Rosalind B. "The Ecological Structure of Negro Homicide." American Journal of Sociology, 67 (1962).

Phillips, G. Howard. Crime in Rural Ohio: Final Report. Wooster: Ohio Agricultural Research and Development Center, 1975.

Polk, Kenneth. "Juvenile Delinquency in Non-metropolitan Areas." In the Presidents Task Force on Law Enforcement and Administration of Justice: Juvenile Delinquency and Youth Crime. Washington, D.C.: U.S. Government Printing Office, 1967.

Porterfield, Austin. "Indices of Suicide and Homicide by States and Cities: Some Southern-non-Southern Contrasts with Implications for Research." American Sociological Review, 14 (1949).

Poveda, Tony G. "The Fear of Crime in a Small Town." Crime and Delinquency, 18 (1972). Reprinted in Bruce Cohen, Ed. Crime in America. Itasca, IL: F.E. Peacock Publishers, Inc., 1977.

Quinney, Richard. "Structural Characteristics, Population Areas, and Crime Rates in the United States." The Journal of Criminal Law, Criminology and Police Science, 57 (1966).

Redfield, H.V. Homicide, North and South: Being a Comparative View of Crime Against the Person in Several Parts of the United States. Philadelphia: Lippincott, 1880.

Schultz, LeRoy. "The Rural Social Worker and Corrections." In Leon Ginsberg (Ed.), Social Work in Rural Communities. New York: Council on Social Work Education, 1976.

Shannon, Lyle W. "The Spatial Distribution of Criminal Offenses by States." Journal of Criminal Law, Criminology and Police Science, 45 (1954).

Shaw, Clifford, et al. Delinquency Areas. Chicago: University of Chicago Press, 1929.

Smith, Bruce. Rural Crime Control. New York: Columbia University Press. 1933.

Smith, Mapheus. "Tier Counties and Delinquency in Kansas." Rural Sociology, 2 (1937).

Sorokin, P., Zimmerman, Carle C., and Galpin, Charles J. A Systematic Sourcebook in Rural Sociology. Minneapolis: University of Minnesota Press, 1930. (See pp. 266-303. Note an especially good bibliography here of studies from many European nations relevant to rural crime.)

Srole, Leo. "Social Integration and Certain Corollaries: An Exploratory Study." American Sociological Review, 21 (1956).

Steffensmeier, Darrell J. and Jordan, Charlene. "Changing Patterns of Female Crime in Rural America, 1962-1975." Rural Sociology, 43 (1978).

United States Department of Justice. Uniform Crime Reports 1976. Washington, D.C.: U.S. Government Printing Office, 1977.

Warner, John R., Jr. Rural Crime: a Bibliography. Monticello, IL: Vance Bibliographies, 1978.

Webb, Sidney and Beatrice. English Local Government: The Story of the King's Highway. New York: Longmans, 1913.

Wiers, Paul. "Juvenile Delinquency in Rural Michigan." Journal of Criminal Law and Criminology, 32 (1939).

Wirth, Louis. "Urbanism as a Way of Life." The American Journal of Sociology, 44 (1938).

Yoke, H.L. "Crime in West Virginia." Sociology and Social Research, 16 (1932).

CHAPTER III

JUVENILE JUSTICE: A RURAL-URBAN COMPARISON

by Edward J. Pawlak

The main purpose of this chapter is to describe the handling of juvenile offenders by urban and rural juvenile courts. Specifically, urban and rural courts are compared in terms of the percentage of juveniles who receive informal hearings, diagnostic services and institutional dispositions. In order to determine whether urban and rural courts handle different kinds of juveniles, the percentage of recidivists and different types of offenders are also compared. In addition, the size of the judiciary and probation staff and the volume of referrals are compared in order to understand the demands on and resources of urban and rural courts.

Data and Methodology

The author had access to a large pool of data originally collected for official purposes--over 97,000 cases in 66 county juvenile courts in one state from 1966 to 1968 (Note 1). A state research and planning agency provided data that were originally obtained from standard reporting forms completed by probation officers for every referral for which a disposition was reached.

The measurement or classification of counties (and courts) as rural or urban is a difficult task. One can use criteria such as county population size, the percentage of urban population or of people employed as farmers, etc. However, there are problems inherent in the use of any of these measures. A county's population may be small, but it may have one or more dominant small or medium-sized cities that make the county more urban than rural. Or a county may be at a midpoint in its transition from a rural to an urban place. The U.S. Bureau of Census defines urban as locations with 2,500 or more people. Two counties with 35,000 people may be classified as having the same percentage of urban population, but one county may have a dominant central place with 25,000 people and the other county may have 10 urban areas each with 2,500 people. The percentage of farm workers in a county may serve as an indicator of ruralness. However, the purposes of this study require a measure of the character of counties that is more than an indicator of an agricultural economy.

Fortunately, the state in which these courts are located developed a classification system based on county population size which also serves as a means of determining state budgetary allocations to the counties. Thus, the juvenile courts were grouped into eight classes according to the state's classification of counties in order to place the courts on a rural-urban continuum. Census data were examined to identify the mean percentage and the range of the urban population in each class to provide another indicator of the urban character of the class. Table 1 (on the following page) shows the number of courts in each class, the mean percentage and the range of urban population, and the population range of each class. The data in Table 1 suggest that the classification is a reasonably reliable indicator of the urban-rural continuum. County Class 8 is the most rural class and County Class 1 is the most urban. Most of the attention in this paper is focused on the 38 courts in Classes 6, 7, 8--the most rural courts.

TABLE 1

Number of Courts in County Classes, Mean Percentage and Range Of Urban Population, and Population of Counties in Each Class

County Class	No. of Courts in Class	Percent Urban[a] Mean	Percent Urban[a] Range	Population
8	9	11	00-42	20,000
7	13	22	0-47	20-45,000
6	16	33	14-47	46-95,000
5	7	58	43-71	95-149,000
4	10	59	33-80	150,000-249,000
3	9	68	30-87	250,000
2	1	94	-----	over one million
1	1	100	-----	approx. two million

[a]The U.S. Bureau of Census definition of urban is used: location with 2,500 or more people.

Volume of Referrals

The most obvious difference between urban and rural courts is the volume of referrals. Table 2 shows that the most rural courts in Classes 7 and 8 had very few referrals, while the volume of referrals in the two most urban courts was staggering. Several of the largest urban courts individually had more referrals in one month than many of the rural courts combined

TABLE 2

Number and Range of Delinquency Referrals Processed by Juvenile Courts By County Class: 1966-1968

County Class	No. of Courts in Class	Total Referrals	Range of Referrals
8	9	243	8-80
7	13	1,715	2-416
6	16	4,636	49-652
5	7	4,350	169-1,311
4	10	13,294	817-1,869
3	9	13,434	445-3,955
2	1	18,106	18,106
1	1	41,907	41,907
State			97,685

had in three years. Sixteen rural courts within Classes 6, 7, and 8 had fewer than 85 referrals in three years.

One rural informant suggested that the volume of referrals in rural courts would have been smaller, but the juvenile court is often the only resource capable of handling an offender. Whatever the case may be, the data in Table 2 reveal the difficulty rural areas experience in justifying and establishing programs for a small number of rural youthful offenders. Regional programs that encompass several counties and that require intergovernmental planning and cooperation are obviously necessary.

Judges and Probation Officers

The juvenile court is a county court and it is a part of another court system except in the two largest counties. The largest county has a family court and the second largest county has an independent juvenile court in which the judge, who presides only in this court, is elected to his judicial post by the voters of the county. In the largest county, 16 judges are elected to serve the metropolitan court and the presiding judge assigns 10 judges to serve the juvenile court. In the other counties, the judges are elected and they serve concurrently as judges of several county courts. In smaller and rural counties, the same judge presides in all courts. In counties with more than one judge, the presiding judge assigns the judges to juvenile court. Assignment patterns vary from county to county. Certain judges are more or less permanently assigned to preside in juvenile court and they acquire an identity and a reputation as the juvenile court judge. In other counties, all of the judges preside in a juvenile court on a rotating basis, or for a fixed period of time. Full-time juvenile court judges are the exception rather than the rule.

Judges are apportioned to judicial districts which are coterminous with county political boundaries. However, in eight instances two counties have been combined into one judicial district and are served by the same judge. The number and kinds of judges apportioned to a jurisdiction are based on the size of the county's population.

Table 3 (on the following page) shows the number of jurisdictions that have one judge, two judges, etc. The deployment of the judiciary is described here in order to call attention to the variation in structure and in modes of operation among county juvenile courts. The table shows that there are 30 jurisdictions that have only one judge, which means that each judge serves concurrently as judge of all of the county courts. All of these jurisdictions are in Classes 6, 7, and 8. Typically, there are no fixed juvenile court sessions in these jurisdictions, but rather juvenile court cases are scheduled when an opening is available in the court calendar, or at the judge's convenience.

Probation departments are administrative units of the county juvenile court and each county probation department is autonomous. [In some states probation services are a component of state-administered corrections programs.] Probation officers are selected by the juvenile court judges in each county. In large courts a chief probation officer is appointed to supervise the probation staff and to assure the maintenance of probation standards.

TABLE 3

Distribution of Judges in County Court Jurisdictions: January 1969

	Number of Judges							
	1	2	3	4	5	6	9	Total[a]
Number of Jurisdictions	30	8	8	5	2	3	1	57

[a]There are 59 jurisdictions in this eastern state. The two largest urban counties are not included for the reasons indicated in the text above.

Table 4 shows the number of counties that have one probation officer, two probation officers, etc. The table shows that most of the probation departments are very small in size. Of the 10 counties about which data are not available, seven probably have one or less probation officers inasmuch as they have 50 or less referrals per year. Thus, in approximately 50 percent of the courts, the probation department is a one-person or less operation.

TABLE 4

Distribution of Probation Staff Among County Juvenile Courts: December 1969

	Size of Probation Staff									
	1[a]	1[b]	2[c]	3[d]	4-5	6-7	9	50	125	Total
Number of Counties	10	17	7	6	5	7	2	1	1	56[e]

[a]Ten counties do not have full-time probation officers.

[b]Includes four counties that have less than two officers but more than one officer; i.e., 1¼ and 1½.

[c]Includes one county that has 2½ officers.

[d]Includes one county that has 2-3/4 officers and two counties that have 3½ officers.

[e]Data for 10 counties are not available.

Juvenile courts vary in their structure and in their complexity and much of this variation is related to the volume of referrals and to the urban or rural character of the county. The size of the probation staff and the judiciary ranges from two-person operations in rural and less populous counties to complex organizations with large staffs in more populous and urban counties. In many rural courts neither the judge nor the probation officer perform their roles on a full-time basis. Approximately 50 percent of the state's juvenile courts are staffed by two people, a judge and a probation officer, and all of these courts are in the most rural areas. This raises questions about the ability of courts in rural or small communities to attract qualified personnel. Who wants to work in a one-person department with little or no professional or collegial supervision? There are few opportunities for shared decision making or for peer review on such matters as social studies, diagnostic evaluations, treatment strategies and dispositional recommendations.

The coordination of various internal units of the court becomes more complex as the size of the judiciary and the court increases. Courts must develop mechanisms to control the use of discretion and to deal with competing professional ideologies and commitments (Note 2). Consequently, urban courts may rely on standardization and other bureaucratic mechanisms to control the processing of juveniles and the relations among the internal units of the court. Interorganizational linkages and arrangements between the court and other organizations also vary from court to court. Urban courts have differentiated and specialized internal units to manage interorganizational relations. On the input side, intake staff are assigned to deal with referrals from other organizations. Court staff may specialize in drug abuse, status offenses or diagnostic evaluations. On the output side, probation staff are assigned to facilitate the processing of institutional commitments or supervise community placements. In rural courts one person typically handles all of these functions. This suggests that rural areas need highly qualified, mature staff who can serve several functions and who can work independently. The difficulty in finding qualified personnel is aggravated by the political and social character of certain rural areas where political considerations influence probation officer appointments, or where the social structure of "friends and neighbors" calls for the appointment of a "home-grown good ol' boy" rather than an "outsider."

These variations in structure and complexity raise questions concerning the processing of juveniles and their dispositions. Do judges who spend a considerable amount of time in juvenile court have different dispositions than judges who preside infrequently in juvenile court? Judges who frequently preside in juvenile court may have more knowledge of delinquency, juvenile court law and the correctional system, and consequently they may have different dispositions. Judges who preside infrequently in juvenile court may be more dependent on the probation staff for dispositional recommendations. In rural areas, court officials may interact with offenders and their families in several social contexts outside of the court (church, school), or court staff may "know the family." Thus, court staff and offenders' families may be part of the same social network. The influence of such ties on the handling of juveniles in rural courts is unknown. In any case, power and dependence relationships between the judges and court staff, and between court staff and offenders' families, may vary from court to court and these variations may have consequences for the processing of juveniles.

Recidivists and Types of Offenders

Do urban and rural courts handle different kinds of offenders? Table 5 shows that rural courts handle a larger percentage of first offenders and that, overall, urban courts handle more recidivists. Most of the differences are among juveniles with at least one prior court contact. However, both rural and urban courts have a similar percentage of juveniles with two or more prior contacts. The most dramatic differences are between the largest urban court and all of the other classes including other urban courts.

It is not surprising that rural counties have a larger percentage of first offenders. There are limited resources for diversion in rural areas and petitioners and complainants must resort to referral of first offenders to the juvenile court.

TABLE 5

Prior Court Contacts of Juveniles Among County Juvenile Courts by County Class (Percent)[a]

County Class	Prior Court Contacts			
	None	One	Two or More	Total
8	70	12	15	243
7	78	12	9	1,715
6	70	15	10	4,636
5	71	14	13	4,350
4	60	20	19	13,294
3	65	19	15	13,434
2[b]	--	--	--	18,106
1	39	42	11	41,907

[a]Unknown and special proceedings are excluded.

[b]This court's measure of prior court contacts was not reliable and it was excluded from the analysis.

Table 6 (on the following page) shows that the two most urban courts handle a larger percentage of juveniles who commit crimes against persons and a larger percentage of victimless crimes than the rural classes of courts or the other urban classes of courts. Even the other urban classes of courts (3, 4) handle a larger percentage of such crimes than the four rural classes of courts, but the differences are not as marked. Overall, the rural courts handle a larger percentage of property crimes than the urban courts, but again the marked differences are between the most rural and the most urban classes. With the exception of the largest urban court, the percentage of juvenile code offenders handled by the urban and rural class of courts are similar. These patterns are not surprising. According to several rural informants, the opportunity structure for crimes of violence against persons and drug and sex related crimes is a feature of urbanization. At the same time, however, a rural informant who directs a drug abuse program in a rural area reported that there is more drug abuse in rural areas than people realize or are willing to admit, and alcohol abuse is also a problem.

TABLE 6

Reasons for Referral of Juveniles Among County Juvenile Courts by County Class (Percent)[a]

County Class	Offense Type				
	Persons	Property	Victimless	Juvenile	Total
8	3	54	5	25	243
7	4	61	5	22	1,715
6	4	52	6	29	4,636
5	5	55	7	25	4,350
4	7	46	12	29	13,294
3	6	53	8	27	13,434
2	10	45	19	22	18,106
1	17	39	19	16	41,907

[a]Other and unknown are excluded.

Informal vs. Formal Hearings

At the same time or shortly after the court decides to detain or release an alleged offender, the probation staff conducts an investigation to determine the kind of handling a case should receive. The staff determines whether a case warrants juvenile court action or whether a case is outside of its jurisdiction. If a case is within the jurisdiction of the court, it has two alternatives: the court may handle a case informally or formally. In an informal hearing, a case is reviewed by the court's probation department for correctional or referral services. If a case receives a formal hearing, a petition is filed with the clerk of the juvenile court and the case is adjudicated at a hearing before a judge who makes an official disposition of the case.

The imbalance between the volume of referrals and court staff resources, and the fact that most judges preside in other courts, creates a condition wherein formal hearings must be rationed. A system of priorities for the allocation of formal hearing capacity is essential if the court is to be effectively and efficiently managed. Court staff must be selective in screening juveniles for formal hearings. Consequently, the differential selection of offenders for informal hearings among urban and rural courts merits analysis.

In order to facilitate analysis (see Table 7 on the following page), the eight classes were subdivided into two categories--rural (8, 7, 6, 5) and urban (1, 2, 3, 4). Ten of the 45 rural courts (22 percent) have informal

TABLE 7

Number of Courts in Each Class That Have Similar Rates of Informal Hearings

County Class	No. of Courts in Class	Percentage of Informal Hearings									
		Mean	0-10	11-20	21-30	31-40	41-50	51-60	61-70	71	Total
8	9	9	6	1	1	-	-	-	-	1	243
7	13	49	6	2	1	1	1	-	-	2	1,715
6	16	40	5	-	3	2	1	2	1	2	4,636
5	7	40	2	2	1	-	-	1	1	-	4,350
4	10	66	1	-	1	-	-	1	1	6	13,294
3	9	38	3	-	-	3	-	2	1	-	13,434
2[a]	1	-	-	-	-	-	-	-	-	-	18,106
1	1	25	-	-	1	-	-	-	-	-	41,907
State	66	44	23	5	8	6	2	6	4	11	97,685

[a]Data were not available.

hearings for 51 percent or more of the juveniles. Eleven of the 21 urban courts (52 percent) have informal hearings for 51 percent or more of the juveniles. Thus, rural courts are more likely to rely on formal hearings for most of their juvenile offenders. Twenty-four of the 28 courts that handle 20 percent or less of their cases informally are rural courts (see Columns 4 and 5, Table 7).

Diagnostic Services

Diagnostic services include psychiatric, psychological and social work services, provided alone or in any combination to juveniles in order to facilitate treatment recommendations or dispositions. The purpose of this section is to explore whether there are any differences among urban and rural class courts in the percentage of juveniles who receive diagnostic services.

Table 8 (on the following page) shows that 10 of 19 urban class courts (52 percent) provided diagnostic services to 50 percent or more of its juveniles. Twelve of 45 rural class courts (26 percent) provided diagnostic services to 50 percent or more of its juveniles. This pattern is not surprising. Diagnostic services are expensive and scarce, and are more likely to be available in urban areas. One state informant reported that a few courts in rural areas adjacent to a university take advantage of such a resource to obtain diagnostic services.

Institutionalization

Juvenile courts are involved in a vast and complicated interorganizational network that includes public and private agencies in social welfare, in mental health, and in mental retardation on the local, county and state level. Some of these resources are not equally available to all counties. All counties have the right to use state-owned resources. However, the geographic remoteness of the state resource to the county may make the resource inaccessible or not in the best interests of the offender. Also, certain rural counties do not have the kinds of local private services that are usually available in urban counties. Thus, rural social workers are interested in determining how rural courts resolve the placement dilemma. Although there are several types of final disposition, the main interest here is a comparison of the percentage of juveniles who are institutionalized in urban and rural class courts.

Table 9 (on page 47) shows that most urban class courts have placement rates that cluster around the state mean of 12 percent. There is more variation in the percentage of juveniles who are institutionalized among rural class courts than among urban class courts. Among rural courts (Classes 6, 7, and 8) both extremes are represented--the lowest and the highest percentage of institutionalization. Otherwise, there are no clear urban-rural distinctions.

Rural informants and state officials offered contradictory interpretations of the rural data in Table 9 that parallel the variation in the table itself. One informant reported that rural judges are unlikely to commit a son or daughter of a local family to a distant institution. He said, "We like to take care of our own." Yet, others reported that the lack of facilities in rural areas leads to inappropriate reliance on institutional placements.

TABLE 8

Number of County Juvenile Courts with Similar Rates Of Provision of Diagnostic Services

County Class	No. of Courts in Class	Percent of Juveniles Receiving Diagnostic Services									
		Mean	0-10	11-20	21-30	31-40	41-50	51-60	61-70	71	Total
8	9	13	4	2	1	-	1	-	-	-	243
7	13	19	7	2	-	-	-	-	2	2	1,715
6	16	40	4	3	2	3	-	-	2	2	4,636
5	7	45	4	-	-	-	-	-	1	2	4,350
4	10	43	3	-	1	-	1	2	1	2	13,294
3	9	34	4	1	-	-	-	3	-	1	13,434
2[a]	1	-	-	-	-	-	-	-	-	-	18,106
1	1	14	-	1	-	-	-	-	-	-	41,907
State			26	8	4	3	2	5	6	9	97,685

[a]Data were not available.

TABLE 9

Number of Courts in Each Class That Similar Rates
Of Institutionalization

County Class	No. of Courts in Class	Percent Institutionalized							Total Referrals
		Mean	0-4	5-9	10-14	15-20	21-30	30	
8	9	18	2	3	2	-	1	1	243
7	13	8	5	2	1	2	1	2	1,715
6	16	12	-	7	4	2	3	-	4,636
5	7	9	2	3	1	1	-	-	4,350
4	10	9	1	6	3	-	-	-	13,294
3	9	13	-	2	2	2	3	-	13,434
2	1	8	-	1	-	-	-	-	18,106
1	1	14	-	-	1	-	-	-	41,907
State	66	12	10	24	14	7	8	3	97,685

Recapitulation and Discussion

Urban courts have a large volume of referrals and in the largest urban court the volume of referrals is staggering. Many urban courts have as many referrals in one month as several rural courts combined have in three years. In the face of such numbers, one can understand the difficulty rural areas have in making a compelling case for resources. Approximately one-half of the juvenile courts have part-time judges who also preside in other courts, and one or a fraction of one probation officer. Thus, virtually all of the rural courts are, at best, two-person departments. Overall, rural courts handle more first offenders and juveniles who commit property crimes than urban courts; urban courts handle a larger percentage of juveniles who commit victimless and person crimes than rural courts.

Although there is variation within both urban and rural class courts in the percentage of juveniles who receive informal hearings and diagnostic services, one can make the generalization that more rural courts have more formal hearings than urban courts, and that more urban courts provide more diagnostic services than rural courts.

There are no clear rural-urban distinctions in the percentage of juveniles who are institutionalized, other than the fact that rural courts have both extremes of the continuum--the highest and the lowest percentage of institutionalization.

The volume of referrals and the size of court staff in rural areas suggest that intergovernmental planning and cooperation are essential if rural youthful offenders are to have access to programs and services. The small volume of referrals precludes the establishment of detention facilities or community-based facilities in each county. Regional development of programs and facilities will limit the placement of youthful offenders with adult offenders in county jails. In some states, programs administered at the state level are decentralized into development districts or regions of the state. Some counties within a region cooperate by developing a regional detention and diagnostic center. Thus, a qualified pool of professional staff can be made available to juvenile courts. Professional staff can serve rural areas and still be part of a professional collegium rather than professionals working in isolation.

This report has several limitations. In a few instances, the data are merely presented with little interpretation; explanations are very tentative, ad hoc speculations. However, the main purpose of this exploratory, descriptive study is to discern whether different patterns of processing offenders exist among urban and rural juvenile courts. The character of this study--secondary analysis of data originally collected for official purposes--did not permit pursuit of definitive explanations or interpretation of the data.

When a study lacks closure, it is customary to end on a hopeful note and this author intends to maintain the tradition. The value of the study is that it describes and compares some of the resources and practices of urban and rural courts. Hopefully, this study will spur others to pursue the matter further.

NOTES

1. The identity of the state and county juvenile courts is withheld at the request of state officials. This is one of the few states that has a centralized repository of county juvenile court data. Thus, it is not necessary to approach each court individually in order to obtain data about their operating modes and clients. The use of official data in organizational analysis allow for a longitudinal and comparative perspective. The time and money that would be required to duplicate the data-gathering efforts of official agencies would prohibit or seriously limit such research. However, official data have shortcomings. In this case, the data were not made available until late in 1969. It took one year to de-bug the tapes, recode the data and to write a new computer program that could process over 90,000 cases efficiently. The data had to be accepted without certain information about clients and about the courts that would have enhanced the analysis. One has to balance the above disadvantages with the advantages of having a considerable amount of data about many organizations.

2. William C. Brennan and Shanti Khinduka, "Role Expectations of Social Workers and Lawyers in the Juvenile Court," Crime and Delinquency, 17 (April), 191-201; George Kelling and Quentin F. Schenk, "Stresses Accompanying the Professionalization of Corrections," Crime and Delinquency, 17 (October), 355-372; Chester Bartoo, "Some Hidden Factors Behind a Probation Officer's Recommendations," Crime and Delinquency, 9 (July), 276-281; Shirley McCune and Daniel S. Koler, "Juvenile Court Judges in the United States: A National Profile," Crime and Delinquency, 2 (April), 121-131.

CHAPTER IV

CRIME, DELINQUENCY AND CRIMINAL JUSTICE SERVICES IN RURAL AMERICA

by H. Wayne Johnson

Conspicuous by its absence in the emerging rural social services literature is an examination of the problems of crime, delinquency and correctional programs. This absence of attention to these social problems and programs on the rural scene should not be surprising. There is the image of clean air, green countryside, a crime-free rural America in contrast to corrupt, wicked, crime-ridden urban centers.

Any rural dweller can testify to the inaccuracy of this picture in view of rising rates of crime and delinquency in these areas of the nation. Rustling of livestock, theft of equipment, burglary of farm and small town homes, and vandalism are only some of the criminal acts confronting rural residents.

What do the statistics show? While record keeping in the crime and delinquency field in the United States leaves much to be desired, the best information available makes it quite clear that there is reason for concern, rather than complacency, relative to such deviancy in the rural community. Although there continues to be more crime and a higher rate of illegal activity in the cities, the growth of crime is greater in nonmetropolitan areas. For example, FBI Uniform Crime Reports for the year 1976 compares the arrest rate for cities, suburban, and rural areas yearly from 1972 through 1976. While the urban rate remained fairly constant, with only a slight drop over this period, the rate for rural areas showed a marked and steady increase every year except for 1975-76 when it was almost constant. The suburban arrest rate, higher than the rural but lower than the urban, was more erratic over these five years with an overall modest increase.[1]

Youth and young adults play a large part in the nation's crime. However, according to the FBI report, the distribution of arrests were lower for the younger age groups in rural areas.[2] Juvenile Court Statistics, another federal source of information, indicates that in 1974 urban juvenile court cases (in contrast to arrests) increased by 11 percent over the previous year and semi-urban cases increased by 3 percent, whereas rural juvenile court cases increased by 15 percent.[3] The increase of juvenile cases in rural courts is associated more with male than female delinquency.[4] It is seen then that whichever measure is used, arrests or juvenile court cases, rural America is not free of offenders. It does enjoy a comparatively favorable situation in contrast to the cities and suburbs, but change is present and crime may be increasing more rapidly in the rural parts of the nation.

Three major subsystems constitute the criminal justice system regardless of community size: law enforcement, justice, and corrections. In rural enti-

---

[1]Federal Bureau of Investigation, Uniform Crime Reports. (Washington, D.C., 1977), p. 171.

[2]Ibid., p. 172.

[3]U.S. Department of Justice, Juvenile Court Statistics, 1974. (Washington, D.C., 1977), p. 5.

[4]Ibid., p. 6.

ties, the usual characterizations of these groups apply along such lines as lack of resources, relative isolation and small size, along with the attendant limitations.

There are problems and potentialities in each of these three subsystems. The intent here is to be suggestive rather than exhaustive in relation to some of the possibilities for program and policy development. In the case of law enforcement in the rural community, the major lines of defense are municipal police, constables and marshals on one hand, and the county sheriff system on the other. Various means of strengthening rural law enforcement have occurred over the past decade due to a number of developments, but particularly resulting from efforts of the Law Enforcement Assistance Administration (LEAA). As a result, rural law enforcement is more sophisticated and advanced than ever before.

One of the more recent innovations has been police social work, due primarily to the pioneering efforts of Professor Harvey Treger at the University of Illinois, Chicago. The idea is to team social workers with police personnel in order to solve problems such as domestic disputes and youth difficulties frequently encountered by police.

What is noteworthy from the perspective of the present discussion is that almost all of the social work/police activity thus far has been in small cities. Illinois has been the site of most of this development in the nation, beginning in such communities as Wheaton and Niles, each with about 31,000 population.[5] While these are suburbs of Chicago, a social worker in Iowa is already employed by the police department in a community of 20,000 and consideration of such a program is currently underway in a community with a population of only 6,000.

The possibilities of strengthening the human service system would appear to be considerable with the addition of social work to law enforcement and the blending of these two endeavors. In general, the kind of social worker required in this context in the rural area would be a competent generalist with strong clinical skills.

One of the major developments, particularly in the judicial arena today, is diversion, or providing alternative programming for the accused or convicted offender to route him or her away from the consequences traditionally flowing from deviancy. Through diversion it is hoped to avoid the often damaging results of incarceration or other destructive aspects of processing in the usual court, probation, incarceration, or parole experience. Diversion can be designed for nonpopulous communities. An Iowa county of 72,000 population has just instituted a juvenile diversion program which is aimed at early diversion, i.e. prior to the filing of delinquency petition by the county attorney's office. This model is readily adaptable to much smaller counties. Two or more adjacent counties could jointly carry out this program effectively.

Thirdly, corrections present perhaps the greatest number of challenges and opportunities within the criminal justice spectrum. Every rural area is served by both juvenile and adult probation and parole in some way, even if

---

[5]Harvey Treger, "Wheaton-Niles and Maywood Police-Social Service Projects," Federal Probation. September, 1976, pp. 33-39.

it is by one overworked agent serving several counties at considerable distance. The need is for qualified and adequately paid staff to serve a geographical area of reasonable size with caseloads that are not excessive. While this seems utopian in some parts of the country, progress is being made in many areas.

The institutional aspect of corrections deserves special comment. A traditional part of our societal response to criminality has been and continues to be the county jail and town lock-up. Some of these structures are among the most obsolete and deplorable in relation to physical inadequacy and a dearth of any meaningful programming for inmates. Each facility needs to be assessed singly to ascertain whether it should be razed or modernized. Such decisions should be made in the context of a total integrated state plan for detention, short term incarceration and the role of the jail. Most states will find that they have more jails than needed as we move toward the twenty-first century. Regional facilities may at least be a partial answer. Whatever directions are ultimately taken, it is paradoxical to contemplate the most local of all correctional (penal) facilities in an era in which "community-based corrections" has become a popular phrase in some professional circles.

Juveniles present a serious problem because based on the standards of such organizations as the National Council on Crime and Delinquency, very few should be detained in jail. Most specialized separate juvenile detention centers are in metropolitan communities. It is not surprising that a considerable number of rural youths find themselves detained in places such as the county jail. The inappropriateness of such placements is testified to by all too frequent suicides and other tragedies accompanying the jailing of youth. Detention is overused for juvenilves, both rural and urban. Part of the answer, then, is a reduction in the amount of detention. Other partial solutions in rural areas are multi-county regional detention facilities, greater use of temporary foster care on a highly individualized basis and group shelter care homes. With the latter, extra consideration may need to be given to security features without converting a home to a bastile. This has been done in some communities and can be done in others.

State training schools for juveniles, and penitentiaries and reformatories for adults, are longer-term institutions. Interestingly many, if not most, of these facilities are located in rural areas, although today they are largely populated by urban offenders. Not only are they not in a city, they are not even within the boundaries of a small community. Rather, they are often on the edge of a town or located entirely out in the country. Like many state mental hospitals, their remote locations put the "client" group out of sight and out of mind of the general populace. Often these facilities include a farm. Therefore employees of such institutions, including social workers and counselors, are often rural dwellers.

The need today is for diversity in programming and deinstitutionalization.

The nation is experiencing a building boom in prisons at the very time it should be developing genuine community-based, noninstitutional programs. For example, in Iowa, a rural state, a recent plan recommends the expenditure of $55 million over five years to "upgrade the corrections system." The question is what form this upgrading will take. If most of it goes for brick, mortar and steel to construct institutions that are exhorbitantly expensive to erect and maintain and destructive to the persons to be "served," it is money poorly spent. Legislators should consider very carefully what this money could purchase in community-based programs such as a system of smaller, less architecturally secure institutions with a diversity of objectives, release centers and half-way houses with an emphasis on education, training, and employment, programs of partial confinement, restitution or community service. The focus should be, then, on deinstitutionalization and the provision of alternatives.

Returning to juvenile delinquency again, there are many possibilities for developing services in the rural community. Group homes are one promising resource that can be established even in very small communities. A variety of structural and administrative arrangements are available for such programming.

In 1976 another program was created in Iowa to fill the human services gap for rural youth. It was entitled the "Career Development Program" (CDP). As of 1977, 75 percent of the 500 youths in this self-help program were from communities of under 8,000. Amost all were dropouts and about half had been in trouble with the law. The program is for youth aged 16 to 21 and promotes career exploration development, academic opportunity and job training.[6]

A Washington, D.C. consultant to the program observed, "Generally rural areas are a wasteland as far as resources for youth with special needs are concerned. The small town kids I met in Iowa were among the most emotionally battered I've seen anywhere in the country. In cities, youngsters usually have a peer group--if only a street gang--to identify with. It's not so easy in small towns." A successful graduate of the program said, "Once a small town kid gets a bad reputation, it's almost impossible to shake it no matter what you do. . .the county sheriff was one of the few who tried to help me."[7]

The last program innovation that will be mentioned, which is compatible with the rural scene, is also flourishing in rural Iowa. In-home or family-based care is being used by the State Department of Social Services as well as some private organizations with contracts with the state. Families, Inc. is an example. Located in a small town of 1,300, it serves nine counties, two of which are urban, two semi-urban and the remainder quite rural. In fact, four have county populations of under 20,000. Workers carrying small caseloads invest heavily in families in which at least one child is headed toward institutionalization in the absence of substantial intervention. Much of the work is in the client's home, often during the afternoons and evenings when the entire family is present. The intensity and continuity of highly individualized service appears to have paid off well in the program.

To conclude, there is crime and delinquency in rural America, contrary to the image. Perhaps contrary to another image, there are also services for families and individuals involved with such deviancy. Opportunities for additional rural programs abound and a few possible directions have been indicated here.

---

[6] Des Moines Register, March 13, 1977.
[7] Ibid.

PART II

CHANGING PATTERNS IN RURAL JUVENILE JUSTICE

Introduction

During the past several years there have been major attempts to reform American juvenile justice practices. National mandates have initiated significant changes such as: more due process protections in juvenile court proceedings; de-criminalization of particular categories of juvenile offenses; separation of youthful from adult offenders; deinstitutionalization of status offenders from youth correctional facilities; and development of more community resources which are not solely identified with traditional juvenile justice agencies.

The above changes have several implications for rural areas. While the consequences may vary somewhat from area to area, some common observations can be made:

> Rural areas being called upon to implement and maintain costly service programs which are typically used in urban settings, e.g. detention facilities;
>
> Children not previously identified as offenders become enmeshed in a system as it develops more formalized and complex units of services;
>
> Implementation of "urban" solutions in rural areas which don't necessarily work in urban areas, either; and
>
> Development of services tends to result in better reporting of delinquency activity; hence, the "delinquency problem" is recognized more than ever before.

The following two chapters explore the rural response to major juvenile justice mandates in two particular states: West Virginia and New Jersey. Chambers and Miner assess the structural elements of the juvenile system in West Virginia and how those various elements often impede the development of effective community responses to youth needs.

Such structural impediments are seen in various ways. First, juvenile justice agencies provide less counseling and support services than are needed by troubled youth. Also, there is a general tendency on the part of these agencies to have less contact with private agencies which provide such services; this results in little or no outside support services. Second, the community is not viewed in terms of its contributions to children's frustrations and problems. Rather, children are often viewed as the sole cause of the delinquency problem. This does not take into consideration to what extent children's problems are influenced and shaped by their families, schools and other community systems.

Third, particularly in rural areas, the labeling of a child by juvenile justice agencies results in a community's negative expecations of that child, regardless of the nature of the offense and other contributing factors. What results is that many times such negative attitudes influence the continuance of deviant behavior.

Jankovic assesses the impact of status offender legislation on five rural New Jersey counties. Her research, which analyzes practices both prior to and after major code changes, looks at the processing of juveniles through courts, pre-dispositional care facilities, training school and other out-of-home commitments. In the five years that have elapsed since the code went into effect, it was found that: community shelters served as effective alternatives to detention facilities in rural/nonmetropolitan areas; status offender legislation did not result in a decrease in complaints disposed of in court; the development of pre-dispositional care facilities resulted in an increase in the number of children placed in such facilities; training school commitments for rural/nonmetropolitan counties increased; and use of other dispositional alternatives, e.g. residential facilities, decreased.

Jankovic also discusses her research findings in the context of basic policy/program issues which impacted these particular counties during their implementation of major code changes at the local level.

CHAPTER V

JUVENILE JUSTICE IN WEST VIRGINIA: A CHANGING LANDSCAPE

by Kristin N. Chambers
and
Edwin J. Miner

This article will explore the status of youth in West Virginia, with particular emphasis on juvenile justice and delinquency prevention systems. Our optimal expectation of youth targeted institutions, polices and laws is that they will reflect first and foremost the best interests of the young people involved. Convenience of enforcement or historical precedents are not, in our judgment, sufficient justification to design or maintain any system. Dr. Robert Hunter of the University of Colorado has described access to desirable social roles and positive labeling as the two crucial variables that can positively influence youth development and delinquency prevention.[1] These factors are seldom operative in programming for youth of this state. Instead, social services, legislative activities, law enforcement agencies and the courts interact in a manner that is crippling to the formation of effective youth development strategies.

Our focus is not on the ills of youth themselves but rather on the structural impediments and flaws that hold the majority of youth services at a primitive level. We do not deny that youth can be a problem for their families or their communities; in fact, self-reported delinquent acts nationwide indicate that 80 percent of <u>all</u> juveniles commit a "couple" of offenses and then stop.[2] Although delinquent behavior is a legitimate social concern, we cannot realistically expect to stop all such behavior. We can, however, design our system interventions so they help rather than damage youth. Although there is no evidence that court, detention and probation prevent or control delinquency--and there is evidence that young people who are processed through the juvenile justice system show increases in delinquent behavior[3]--we continue to focus our energies toward legalistic remedies for the problems we encounter with our youth. The folly of this approach is compounded when it is used to deal with status offenses. [Status offenses are those acts which, if committed by an adult would not be considered deviant, much less criminal. Running away, truancy, curfew violations, and incorrigibility are status offenses.]

There is a tendency to view delinquency, including status offenses, as a discrete set of behaviors which violate clearly delineated social mores and law. These behaviors, or delinquent acts, are held to be objective fact and are produced by concrete psychological, environmental, and social class variables (e.g., poor ego formation, single-parent family, or inadequate socialization). Furthermore, delinquency is believed to result from a relatively recent decline

---

[1]Robert M. Hunter, <u>Managing Human Services</u> (Boulder, Colo.: International City Management Association, 1977), p. 18.
[2]National Association of Counties Research Foundation, <u>Juvenile Delinquency: A Basic Manual for County Officials</u> (Washington: National Association of Counties Research Foundation, 1976), p. 2.
[3]Ibid., p. 5.

in respect for authority and moral rectitude. In fact, there is little evidence to support the claim of any of these viewpoints.

Practically, delinquency prevention has proved to be a difficult concept to operationalize on a nationwide basis and is just as elusive in smaller, more homogeneous environments such as West Virginia. Although it is true that all levels of our social and institutional systems maintain ideas about the nature of juvenile delinquency, formal responsibility for policy, problem definitions, and interventions rests largely on the judicial, law enforcement, legislative, and service delivery systems. These systems retain their influence because of their legitimate authority. It is no surprise, then, that when evaluating the legal, structural, and programmatic efficacy of West Virginia's juvenile justice system these groups exclude themselves as part of the problem. However, there is substantial justification for their inclusion in the problem statement. Essentially, it is these systems which unwittingly perpetuate and exacerbate not only the problem of juvenile delinquency, but also hinder the successful socialization of youth.

We would like to buttress this hypothesis with a brief overview of the historical trends in juvenile delinquency. Our particular emphasis is on the categorization of status offenders.

Children and youth have always indulged in conduct that distresses or threatens other segments of the population.[4] In post-industrial societies, childhood misconduct began to constitute a social problem worthy of public concern. Large amounts of time and resources have been directed toward it in an effort to reduce its incidence. Youths have been incarcerated in formal institutions at least since 1825, when the New York House of Refuge was founded. Young persons were there because of two prevailing attitudes: first, that youths were not competent to make decisions about their lives; and, second, that the state had the responsibility to intercede.

The formation of the Illinois Juvenile Court in 1899 firmly institutionalized these notions by establishing noncriminal procedures for youths who had not committed a criminal act but who were in imminent danger of doing so. In addition to these new procedures, each case was dealt with on an individual basis with consideration for the psycho-social conditions of the youth and his or her family. It was a radical and humanely motivated approach to guide youth without stigmatizing them. The court further established delinquency as a status of potentiality. This status was not based on specific behavioral characteristics that violated a point of law, but rather had its origins in cultural and normative considerations which are operative within a jurisdiction. The structure, policies and procedures of the Illinois Juvenile Court of 1899 have survived intact and are currently in effect in West Virginia.

What has been the effect of the juvenile court as an interventive and remediative system? In 1967, the Presidential Commission on Law Enforcement

---

[4]Gene Kassebaum, Delinquency and Social Policy (Englewood Cliffs: Prentice-Hall, Inc., 1974). p. 73.

and Administration of Justice[5] stated:

> The great hopes originally held for the juvenile court have not been fulfilled. It has not succeeded in rehabilitating delinquent youth, in reducing or stemming the tide of juvenile criminality or in bringing justice and compassion to the child offender.

The juvenile justice system has been found to render less service in the form of counseling and support services to youth than they would have had without contact with it.[6] This is true primarily because the courts and police have little facilitative or cooperative contact with private community-based agencies. Also, by virtue of the intake and referral systems of the court and the often specious grounds for pre-hearing detention (nationwide over 50 percent of delinquency petitions are dismissed before the initial hearing)[7] the court is used as a "dumping ground" by parents and the school system. The effect of this process is that courts are forced to seek legal remedies for problems which are generically outside their domain and which they are poorly equipped to handle. The trend to seek adjudication for social and interpersonal problems overburdens the judiciary and delays or denies those legitimately troubled youth in need of services.

The juvenile justice system also functions under the assumption that the community environment is benign. For example, truancy is a status offense for which a youth may be adjudicated delinquent by a juvenile court. Yet this act is often a rational response to an educational system which does not meet the needs of youth. Running away is also a status offense, although it may be an act of courage and emotional health to leave an abusive family environment. Historically, this behavior has been used by the court to establish de facto evidence for intervention, although common sense suggests a nonjudicial approach. It is difficult, near impossible situation for the court to be an effective advocate when it is also a formidable adversary.

The dichotomous goals of the juvenile system produce serious inconsistencies not only in matters of social service but also in legalistic interpretation and procedure. The adversary process in the American judicial system provides for the resolution of conflict between defendant and plaintiff through an impartial judge and jury. In matters affecting juveniles, however, the defendants are left without advocates. The issue for them is not their guilt but their need for treatment. Even in light of U.S. Supreme Court decisions (re: Gault and Winship) due process remains more of a myth than a reality. The right of a juvenile to an attorney, the right to cross-examine witnesses, and protections against self-incrimination are not firmly established in judicial procedure. Although these rights are granted by statute in West Virginia, the absence of an effective appeals process and judicial oversight committees render these rights academic.

---

[5]President's Commission on Law Enforcement and Administration of Justice, "Task Force Report: Juvenile Delinquency and Crime" (Washington, 1967), p. 7.

[6]Rosemary Sarri and Y. Hasenfeld (ed.), Brought to Justice? Juveniles, the Courts, and the Law (Ann Arbor: National Association of Juvenile Corrections, University of Michigan, 1974), p. 95.

[7]Ibid., p. 101.

There is, however, a far more insidious consequence which, although unintended, tends to create the condition the court was designed to alleviate. The juvenile court, functioning as a social service agency, has adopted a delinquency treatment typology which proceeds from identification of client to intervention to treatment. The possibility has been raised by Schur[8] and others that this approach may have a causative rather than rehabilitative effect. The identification process that operates within the juvenile court setting (either referral from parent, citizen, school, or arrest) imposes labels which characterize individuals as deviant or defective and in need of treatment or correction. These labels cause the youth to be treated differentially not only within the domain of the court but in the community as well. Thus, the label becomes a prophecy which fulfills itself as the youth's self-image conforms to fit these negative expectations.

National attention has been focused on this problem, resulting in the passage of the Juvenile Justice and Delinquency Prevention Act in 1974. As a result of this act, the Law Enforcement and Assistance Administration (LEAA) was granted funds to assist states in a program of deinstitutionalization and decriminalization of status offenders. This was generated by national recognition that locking juveniles away in institutions was not rehabilitative; that remanding status offenders to the same facilities as more serious offenders constituted cruel and unusual punishment; and that community-based programs were more humane, less expensive, and showed promise of greater effectiveness.

Approximately $500,000 per year would have been available to West Virginia had a state plan for deinstitutionalization been submitted to LEAA. However, until July, 1977, West Virginia continued to incarcerate status offenders in such institutions as Pruntytown Industrial School for Boys and Salem Industrial School for Girls. Spurred by a West Virginia Supreme Court of Appeals decision rendered by Justice Neely (Harris vs. Calendine) that institutionalizing status offenders with criminal offenders abridged their rights, the West Virginia legislature amended Chapter 49 of the state's code to bring it into compliance with federal standards.

The most sweeping revisions pertained to status offenders: law enforcement officials could no longer take a young person into custody unless grounds exist for the arrest of an adult in identical circumstances. Although procedures still exist to bring truant and unmanageable behavior matters before the court, law enforcement officials have been stripped of their most immediate power--that of instant incarceration. They were also no longer allowed to house juveniles in jail, even in a juvenile section, unless the young person was being moved to a correctional institution.

Although this legislation brought West Virginia into the 1970s in juvenile justice law, no additional funding was appropriated that would assist in the development of community-based alternatives that are necessary to implement the law. The mechanics of handling status offenders when they need services were not specified. This has resulted in confusion, frustration and resistance to change in rural and urban areas of the state. In many instances the law has simply been ignored.

---

[8]Edwin M. Schur, Radical Non-Intervention: Rethinking the Delinquency Problem (Englewood Cliffs: Prentice-Hall, Inc., 1970).

The 1978 legislature considered revisions of the law despite the fact that there had not been enough time to implement the present law or to evaluate its effectiveness. Complaints came from law enforcement officials who claimed the new law severely limited their effectiveness and from parents who could no longer use the court and detention as an easy means of controlling their children. Many revisions were considered, including outright appeal of the 1977 changes, and/or moving the child's right to court-provided counsel, allowing law enforcement officials to take custody of runaways and adding "failure to respond to a summons" to the definition of delinquent behavior.

The new act, Senate Bill 364, was passed on March 11, 1978, and added both restrictive and liberalizing provisions to the juvenile code. The most noteworthy of the former type is the provision for detention of runaways for 48 hours without a petition and for seven days with a petition. The more favorable changes included broadening the definition of child abuse to include emotional and institutional abuse and the addition of a five-member Juvenile Facilities Review Panel to monitor conditions in juvenile institutions.

Although the opponents of Senate Bill 200 failed to seriously damage the spirit of this law, their intent and the hostile rhetoric which was addressed to juvenile reform is alarming. Nowhere in the criticism or dissatisfaction with the 1977 legislation is there mention that youth are not being well served by the new statutes. The problem with the law was not its impact on the lives of the young people, but the difficult enforcement procedures it imposed on officials of the law, the new constraints it placed on the family, and the responsibility it placed on the community to provide alternative services to youth.

Much of the opposition to the legislation was generated by rural judges and law officers who were unquestionably inconvenienced by the restrictions on where they could hold juveniles and how quickly they must provide a hearing. However, even where alternatives exist, agencies have resisted using them.

Patchwork, a Charleston-based residential shelter for runaways, receives few referrals directly from the court and almost none from police. As Kary Gouge, the project coordinator, explains it, police officers are convinced that young people will go "straight out the back door" rather than accept services voluntarily. However, a check of program statistics over a three-month period indicated that out of 110 youth served, only four left the program in the manner anticipated by law enforcement officials.[9]

By their actions, police have operationalized a myth that youth cannot be trusted to participate in getting the services they need. Although Patchwork has been able to work quite successfully outside the mainstream--and even to expand--Charleston as a community is large enough to permit private, independent organizations to assume functions that were once in the public arena _without_ seriously altering any of its institutions. As long as law enforcement officials, the court, and the social services system remain uncommitted to

---

[9]Interview with Kary Gouge conducted in Charleston, Feb. 16, 1978.

alternative, community-based approaches to youth programming and/or delinquency prevention, enlightened legislation can easily be circumvented.

Entrenched institutions are known for their resistance to change. Youth programming has not been the exception. This is illustrated by several features of the state plan for the Juvenile Justice and Delinquency Prevention Act, submitted to LEAA for funding for fiscal 1978-79.

This is the plan, alluded to above, that is intended to demonstrate the state's willingness and ability to deinstitutionalize status offenders. If approved, this plan will provide the state with $435,200 in federal revenue to implement size program components specified in the plan. These programs are supposed to address the goal of deinstitutionalizing status offenders. The plan states that "...maximum utilization of existing resources will be facilitated through the active participation of personnel from state agencies with delinquency prevention and rehabilitation responsibilities in the State Advisory group."[10]

The six program components described by this document are an odd mix of expensive, specialized services to a small number of youths (development of 16 special foster homes at a price of $105,600; day treatment facilities for a maximum of 48 youths at a cost of $200,000) and vague projects that serve the needs of institutions far more directly than the needs of youth. A prime example of this is the component that would reimburse counties for the costs of transferring youths to specialized detention centers in different counties.

It should be noted that the goal is to separate juveniles from adult criminal populations. However, "Inter-County Detention Transportation" is a highly questionable item in a plan which was intended to deinstitutionalize young people. A more appropriate focus would be the development of community resources and alternatives. This emphasis is entirely missing from the plan except for a program that has as its objective "the identification of the projected need for a variety of alternatives for the prehearing care of youth."[11] Again the focus is at the interface between the youth and the law and what is to be done <u>after</u> the commission of a violation.

A fifth component, the development of a resource center that will assist professionals in locating placements for youths presupposes the validity of exisiting programs to meet the needs of juveniles. It is designed as a state wide service that will primarily serve professionals in the discharge of their responsibilities. The final section of the plan calls for community education and training targeted at junior high school teachers, circuit court judges, and probation officers, and the wider community.

This plan can be divided into two parts: one that offers specialized services to a handful of youths and the other that responds to the predilections of agencies and institutions. None of the projects will assist communities in planning youth development strategies or diverting youths from the

---

[10]Governor's Committee on Crime, Delinquency, Corrections, 1978 FY Juvenile Justice and Delinquency Prevention Plan (Charleston, W.Va.: Governor's Office of Economic and Community Development, 1977), p. 107.
[11]Ibid., p. 146.

juvenile justice system, or preventing delinquency or devising community alternatives for those youths who do need services.

The plan claims to reflect the priorities of a Citizen's Advisory group with "technical assistance" provided by the State Department of Public Welfare. Its content, however, strongly reflects the exigencies of bureaucratic structure. The Department of Public Welfare's "technical assistance" appears to have neutralized the purpose of a citizen's group and substituted the goals of the agency. This illustrates the self-justifying tendencies of established institutions. Enforcement and corrections receive their share; the Department of Public Welfare will obtain an ample portion; and court personnel are given consideration and attention. While there are no actual profits available in this arrangement, resources are distributed in such a way that no substantive changes will be forthcoming.

This is the crux of West Virginia's difficulties in developing sound strategies for dealing with youths. Convenient relationships among the various levels or branches of government and institutions tend to maintain the status quo. Citizen input is extremely difficult to operationalize, especially when it finds no receptive leadership working on the inside.

West Virginia does have influential and well-organized groups (primarily women's groups) that have worked diligently for several years to bring the state's treatment of juveniles into a more enlightened framework. The passage of any liberalizing legislation owes much to their efforts. However, these groups cannot succeed without more widespread, informed support. The Portland State University School of Social Work has published a review of intervention approaches for delinquency which concludes:

> Genuine progress in delinquency prevention cannot occur without community support outside the juvenile justice system. Whatever the merits of a prevention program, if community power groups, legislators, established agencies and police do not want it, it will fail.[12]

Despite this framework of systematic and institutional failure there are now some encouraging developments within West Virginia and the nation. The turmoil of the past five years has resulted in greatly increased awareness and strong evidence that West Virginia is beginning to grapple with the problems of justice for our youth. On a local level, there is a growth of community-based youth-oriented agencies. Ohio County has organized a youth service bureau located at Samaritan House in Wheeling. Likewise, Charleston has developed a youth services agency, the Kanawha Youth Services Council, which has as its objectives the promotion of programmatic alternatives in the community and policy change at the state level. Recently, the Community Council of Kanawha Valley received a grant through the Department of Health, Education, and Welfare and the District 17 Department of Welfare to plan for the development of a Comprehensive Emergency Services System which will

---

[12]Edmund V. Mech, Delinquency Prevention: A Program Review of Intervention Approaches (Portland: Regional Research Institute for Human Services, 1975), p. 81.

provide direct services to children and families in crisis. It will also endeavor to prevent those children from becoming ensnared in the juvenile justice system. Also in Charleston, Patchwork, a residential program, and its outreach and primary prevention component, Checkpoint, are offering significant resources. This organization is providing strong community leadership and innovative alternatives for youth before and after they come into contact with law enforcement agencies. In addition, the Appalachian Research and Defense Fund (Apple-Red) is providing critically needed legal advocacy for the civil rights of youth. Although each organization is providing sorely needed services and is demonstrating the worthiness of alternative approaches, they all (with the exception of Apple-Red) function exclusively in the state's major urban areas. Progress toward securing gains for the large number of West Virginia's rural youth is virtually nonexistent.

At the level of judicial, corrections, and social services institutions there has also been some progress. Youth concerns, through the controversial Senate Bill 200 and the State Supreme Court of Appeals Harris vs. Calledine decision, have become the focus of increasing scrutiny. The existence of conflict is not unusual nor unhealthy. The state has also indicated its manifest intent to participate in the Juvenile Justice and Delinquency Prevention Act and thus opens its doors to greater national attention. West Virginia will gain, by filling the state plan, access to a growing body of youth development technology. An outgrowth of this will be the accumulation of a sorely needed data base which will enable the state to increase its capacity to make informed decisions. The Law Enforcement and Assistance Administration has shown that it is willing to do its part in enforcing the stringent requirements of federal law. This will help to insure that the needs of youth are, in fact, served.

Several critical components are currently absent from the prevailing attitudes and trends in this state. Primarily, West Virginia has not turned the corner toward the recognition that decriminalization and deinstitutionalization are insufficient. The status of youths, their behavior and predictable idiosyncrasies, need to be normalized. There is not an inherent criminal nature within young people that demands exceptionalistic and harshly punitive interventions. In large part, their lives are shaped by the social forces around them and, even more critically, by the institutions that are geared to intervene. When their behavior becomes excessively deviant, they require help. This help, however, is not likely to be found within the institutional configurations that presently exist. The following quote from Herman Mannheim[13] serves to illustrate this point.

> We have made considerable effort to discover what sort of person the offender is and why he has broken the law, and we rack our brains to find out what to do with him...Hardly ever do we pause for a moment to examine critically the contents of that very law the existence of which alone makes it possible for the delinquent to offend against it.

---

[13]Herman Mannheim, Criminal Justice and Social Reconstruction (New York: Oxford Press, 1946), p. 1.

Citizens and professionals alike should begin to realize that the promotion of more humane and effective youth strategies is a complex task. Nor is a clear consensus about how to resolve West Virginia's difficulties likely to emerge in the immediate future. In the interim, we can seek to support and develop alternative programs and interventions while continuing to advocate for the necessary institutional changes.

CHAPTER VI

RURAL RESPONSE TO STATUS OFFENDER LEGISLATION

by Joanne Jankovic

The rationale behind major attempts to de-criminalize status offenses (those offenses which constitute conduct illegal only for children) has been that such offenses should not be considered criminal acts. Behaviors defined as "habitual incorrigibility"--running away, truancy and ungovernability--should not to be treated in the same context as those offenses that are considered similar to crimes commited by adult offenders. Sheridan and Beaser, in their attempts to devise a Model Act for Family Courts, noted:[1]

> It is obvious that such actions on the part of the child, while they may be indicative of the imperative need of the child to receive some type of care or treatment, do not necessarily pose a threat to society. They, therefore, will represent the bulk of cases which can safely be diverted from the juvenile justice system, i.e. referred, prior to the filing of a petition, for service or care to a community agency which is not part of the juvenile justice system.

The results of such efforts have been interesting. First, while some states had already revised their juvenile delinquency legislation for the purposes of developing alternative means of classifying or handling status offenses, Congress enacted the Juvenile Justice and Delinquency Prevention Act of 1974, which required all states to comply with federal mandates regarding the classification and treatment of juvenile offenders. Mandates passed on to each state were the following:

> Deinstitutionalization of status offenders from institutions utilized for the incarceration of delinquents;
>
> Separation of juveniles from incarcerated adults;
>
> Development of community-based alternatives to detention and correctional facilities.

We note that while this legislation required major changes in state codes and practices of juvenile correctional agencies, it did not provide for total removal of status offenders from the jurisdiction of the juvenile courts.

Second, the requirements set forth by the Juvenile Justice and Delinquency Prevention Act of 1974 are a first attempt to establish some uniformity of juvenile codes--historically, codes varied from state to state in their definition of what constituted juvenile offenses and how these offenses were processed and disposed of. The strategy to achieve such uniformity was a simple one--if a state wanted to continue receiving federal assistance for its juvenile programs, it had to comply with federal regulations. Third, there is more debate than ever before as to whether or not status offenders, as a particular category, ought to be removed from the jurisdiction of the juvenile

---

[1]William Sheridan and H. Beaser, Model Acts for Family Courts and State/Local Children's Programs (Washington, D.C.: U.S. Dept. of HEW, Office of Youth Development), pp. 14-15.

court altogether. However, the attempt to de-criminalize status offenses has not addressed the issues of continued labeling of these children. The retention of status offenders in the juvenile justice system has often resulted in their being subjected to harsher treatment than their delinquent counterparts. To give an illustration of this, let me summarize some of the findings of a major statewide study of the juvenile code reform in undertaken by Joseph DeJames and Dale Dannefer:[2]

> Status offenders were more than twice as likely as delinquents to be held in temporary custody.
>
> Status offenders are handled more stringently than delinquents--they are more likely to have their cases adjudicated; they are less likely to have their cases dismissed or informally adjusted; and are more likely to receive probation as a disposition. Additionally, status offenders are more often subjected to other forms of social control than delinquents, e.g. "referral to social agencies," while delinquents are more prone to be "counseled and released."
>
> Female status offenders are more likely than male status offenders to receive stringent treatment at every point of the juvenile justice process. On the other hand, female delinquent offenders received more lenient treatment than their male counterparts.

Additionally, their research concluded parent(s) and schools constitute a large proportion of the filing of status offender complaints--this is not true among delinquents. This was due largely to the fact that status offenders are more likely to be from troubled families. Hence, the court, the juvenile shelter and residential facilities often become dumping grounds for children whose problems are based within the family.

A Brief Background

In 1974, New Jersey enacted a new juvenile code which established a separate category for status offenders. The 1974 legislation and administrative regulations which followed required that status offenders could not be placed in predispositional care facilities which were restrictive. Additionally, counties were required to develop separate shelter facilities because no part of detention facilities could be used for status offenders. Status offenders were designated as "juveniles in need of supervision," or JINS.

At the outset of the new code, certain counties were identified by the state as not in need of the development of shelters per se due to previous data noting that the number of status offenders requiring placement had been extremely low. These counties, identified as less-populated and more rural, had historically experienced low numbers of training school commitments, juvenile detainments, etc. Therefore, it was reasoned that counties could make use of alternative arrangements, such as foster home placements or facilities in other counties, in lieu of developing full-scale programs. The particular counties identified were Cape May, Sussex, Warren, Hunterdon, and Salem.

---

[2]Joseph DeJames and Dale Dannefer, Juvenile Justice in New Jersey (Trenton: Department of Human Serivces, 1977), pp. xix-xxxv.

During the first year of the new code, these counties either engaged in contractual arrangements with other counties or showed no record of JINS in need of pre-dispositional shelter care. Until September 1975, the southern counties in Cape May, Salem and Gloucester utilized the Cumberland County shelter on a contractual basis. In February 1976, Salem County opened its own JINS shelter and entered into contractual arrangements with Gloucester and Cape May Counties. In 1978, Cape May opened its own JINS shelter. Sussex, Hunterdon and Warren counties never developed JINS shelters. All three counties had detention facilities, but under the new code were not allowed to use any part of those facilities for shelter. Warren County officials opposed the Department's policy most adamantly, because they had just constructed a new detention facility which they felt could easily qualify for accepting JINS children, by making a portion of it nonrestrictive in nature. Arrangements for temporary shelter care were made with neighboring counties and through the use of temporary foster homes. The rationale for Cape May and Salem Counties to develop JINS shelters must be considered in light of the fact they did not even have detention facilities for temporary holding of JINS or delinquents. Despite the question as to whether or not there was a need for a facility, there were basic problems involved in using temporary arrangements. For instance, police did not like having to transport both JINS and delinquents across county lines for detention/shelter placements. Also, foster home placements were poor solutions due to the emergency nature of a JINS placement, e.g., in the middle of the night. It was reasoned that it was cheaper in the long run to develop their own facilities because of the high costs of contracting with another county.

In a report by the Task Force on the Juvenile Code in 1977, it was noted:[3]

> Once a county establishes a shelter, the number of juveniles placed from that county usually increases dramatically. This is illustrated in Salem County which opened its shelter in February 1976, and had a 954.5 percent increase in the number of juveniles placed in shelter over the previous year. Once other counties establish their own shelters it could be expected that the total admissions for the state may subsequently increase reflecting increases in these counties.

A major issue here is whether or not these counties had an actual need for a JINS program. Like Salem County, Cape May experienced a substantial increase in JINS pre-dispositional placements, with 114 admissions during 1978, its first year of operation. We note that more often than not, as facilities are developed there was a tendency for them to fill up, with the increased availability of bedspace, regardless of "need." However, the issue is one that is complex.

---

[3]Raymond Castro, Task Force on the Juvenile Code Report on Statistics in Shelter and Detention Facilities, April 6, 1977, pp. 1-2.

First, one may assume that previous data noting that there were low numbers of children being handled in a certain manner may have simply meant that problems had been dealt with in other more informal ways, e.g., not reporting information or utilizing a jail or other lock-up facility. Second, the development of a resource such as a JINS shelter in a rural county may have resulted in meeting more "community" needs than its original purpose. For instance, as earlier mentioned, Cape May and Salem counties do not have detention facilties. Children in need of detention are reportedly sent to another county. Seemingly, it is quite possible that some children who would normally be placed in restrictive pre-dispositional settings are instead being placed in shelter care since under the code, while JINS offenders cannot be placed in facilities for delinquents, there is no reason preventing the placement of delinquents in facilities for status offenders. Thus, the utilization of a facility such as a shelter in a rural county for pre-dispositional care may be far more convenient as well as humane than initially intended. Additionally, the costs for the development of a nonsecure facility would be far less than costs required for a secure lock-up detention center. However, in order for us to understand this issue, we have attempted to analyze the juvenile justice practices of these rural counties both prior to and after the passage of the new statutes, to determine to what extent such practices have remained the same or changed.

Data we have selected for our analysis was made available through regular agency reporting mechanisms--the Administrative Office of the Courts, the Department of Corrections and the Division of Youth and Family Services. Guided by the broad question, "Are children treated any differently as a result of the code changes?", it seemed important to look at those indicators which reflected the processing of juveniles through court, pre-dispositional care facilities, state correctional schools and residential care facilities. Since New Jersey makes significant use of private residential treatment facilities as resources for children experiencing a wide range of problems, it seemed appropriate to include data pertaining to children from rural counties in out-of-home placements.

Court Activities

Overall, complaints disposed of in juvenile and domestic relations courts regarding juvenile offenses has increased in the rural counties from 1971 to 1978 by 54.7 percent, at an average of 7.8 percent per year (see Table 1). One of the most interesting points seems to be that even with the separate differentiation of status offense complaints in 1974, counties did not experience any decreases in delinquency complaints. As might be expected, status complaints have steadily increased since they started to be separately recorded in 1974. While the data for previous court years prior to 1974-75 for JINS complaints was not kept, since that time the number of complaints has increased 74.5 percent, rising from 405 to 727, at an average almost 18 percent per year.

Use of Pre-dispositional Care Facilities

Probably the most significant change in rural county activities regarding the care and handling of juvenile offenders has concerned the use of pre-dispositional care facilities as holding or detaining facilities for children awaiting court disposition. This is largely reflected by our earlier discussion

TABLE 1

Complaints Disposed of in Rural/Nonmetropolitan Courts[1]

(N=5)

	1971-1972[2]	1972-1973[2]	1973-1974[3]	1974-1975	1975-1976	1976-1977	1977-1978	Total	Percent Change
JINS	----	----	161	405	673	850	727	2,816	+351.6%
Delinquent	3,592	4,094	4,063	4,307	4,562	4,813	4,829	30,260	+36.1%
Total	3,592	4,094	4,224	4,712	5,235	5,663	5,556	33,076	+54.7%

Notes:

[1]Data maintained by New Jersey Administrative Office of the Courts on court annual calendar--July-June.

[2]Prior to the 1974 code, JINS complaints were not distinguished from delinquent complaints.

[3]This reflects JINS complaints filed from March-July after enactment of the new code.

of those counties not having facilities to begin with or just having one facility, either a shelter or detention center. Table 2 (on the following page) reflects admissions of children to facilities from 1973 through 1978, both for shelter and detention care. As we noted earlier, certain counties do not have detention centers of their own, but utilize facilities in other counties; hence, the data reflected in the table also refer to children placed in facilities outside that particular county for purposes of pre-dispositional care.

Since 1973, rural counties have experienced a growth in the number of children placed in pre-dispositional care facilities (14.6 percent). Most notably, the increase has been greatest regarding the number of shelter admissions. Counties developing new facilities since the inception of the 1974 code have shown the most substantial increases due largely to the development of those facilities. The requirement that certain children no longer be placed in restrictive settings such as detention centers has resulted in some counties experiencing a reduction in the number of detention admissions. For certain counties, this decline is particularly interesting. While they have their own detention centers, they have not developed shelters and have, for the most part, made only minimal use of out-of-county shelter placements.

In comparing rural county activities with activities of other counties across the state, we found that the five counties showed some similar trends with regard to pre-dispositional placements. While there were general decreases in detention placements, there were nonetheless, significant increases in shelter placements--this was due to the fact that no county, prior to the 1974 code, had a separate shelter facility for pre-dispositional care. Probably the most interesting observation is that there hasn't been a significant decrease in the overall number of children placed in pre-dispositional facilities; rather, there has been a slight increase statewide in the number of children placed in such facilities (2.2 percent). Also, we note shelter statistics may be misleading because, particularly in the rural counties, facilities were developed only within the last couple of years. In contrast, the remaining counties developed programs within the first 18 months of the code being in effect. The operationalization of new programs explains the immediate increases in placements.

Generally, there have not been any dramatic changes in the use of pre-dispositional care facilities in terms of removing some children from the juvenile justice system altogether. However, we do note there has been a significant shift from the primary utilization of one facility, e.g. a detention center, to use of other alternatives, notably the JINS shelter.

Commitments to State Juvenile Correctional Facilities

Data available by county for years previous to the 1974 code changes were not available since the department did not keep it accordingly. However, it seems useful to look at those years since the code changes to see if in fact less children have gone to state facilities. Table 3 (on page 73) denotes juvenile commitments to the state training schools from rural counties. While statewide commitments increased over the three year period by slightly more than 2 percent, commitments from rural counties increased by over 65 percent. Female commitments overall represent less than 17 percent of the total commitments from these counties.

TABLE 2

Comparisons in Pre-dispositional Placement Trends Between Rural Counties and other New Jersey Counties

	1973	1974	1975	1976	1977	1978	Total	Percent Change
Rural Counties								
Detention	1,039	759	672	756	808	862	4,896	-17.0%
Shelter	---	---	74	163	199	329	765	+344.6%
Total	1,039	759	746	919	1,007	1,191	5,661	+14.6%
Other New Jersey Counties								
Detention	13,854	10,541	11,142	10,728	9,879	10,014	66,158	-27.7%
Shelter	---	3,057[1]	4,118	4,351	4,331	4,019	19,876	+31.5%
Total	13,854	13,598	15,260	15,079	14,210	14,033	86,034	+1.3%
All Counties								
Total Detention	14,893	11,300	11,814	11,484	10,687	10,876	71,054	-26.9%
Total Shelter	---	3,057[2]	4,190	4,514	4,530	4,348	20,641	+42.2%
Total	14,893	14,357	16,006	15,998	15,217	15,224	91,695	+2.2%

Sources: State of New Jersey Department of Corrections Detention Monitoring Unit, and Division of Youth and Family Services, Bureau of Licensing.

Notes:

[1]As per 1975-1978, since there were no JINS reported in 1974.

[2]Shelter admissions for 10 months, after implementation of code on March 1.

TABLE 3

Commitment of Juveniles to Correctional Institutions
From Rural/Nonmetropolitan Counties

(N=5)

	1976	1977	1978	Total	Percent Change
Male	36	38	61	135	27.5
Female	6	11	9	26	50.0
Total	42	49	70	161	+66.67

Source: New Jersey Department of Corrections.

Rural county commitment trends exceeded statewide trends considerably; overall state commitments during that period has only increased 2.1 percent, according to Department of Correction reports. However, commitments from the five counties represented less than four percent of the total state commitments during the three years.

Children Placed in Other Facilities by the Division of Youth and Family Services

Out-of-home placement patterns were determined by reviewing quarterly reports prepared by the Division of Youth and Family Services accounting the whereabouts of children under the agency's supervision. These reports do not reflect the number of children placed during a specified period of time, but rather the actual number in a particular place at one time. Quarterly reports for March 31 of each year were used to obtain this data. Calculations were made of those children in placements other than with their own parents or relatives--placements ranged from foster homes to state institutions, as well as out-of-state private facilities.

As we had mentioned earlier, our rationale for looking at placement statistics was largely due to the fact that out-of-home placements such as private schools and institutions are used as major resources for children in need of some type of child welfare service. Additionally, under the juvenile code, the juvenile court judge can exercise the dispositional alternative of placing a child under the care of the Division of Youth and Family Services (DYFS). While DYFS has the authority to determine the appropriate plan of services for the child and/or his family, the court many times takes the prerogative of placing in a court order instructions for residential placement. Also, while JINS since March 1974 could no longer be committed to institutions for delinquents, it could be reasoned that the number of residential placements may have increased as alternatives to state training facility commitments.

Table 4 (on the following page) reflects the number of children in out-of-home placements from 1972 to 1978. Since 1972, the overall number of children in placement has decreased measurably, by 22.4 percent, an average of 3.2 percent per year. Most interesting is the fact that these counties were experiencing decreases prior to the 1974 code (-5.1 percent).

The most substantial decline in out-of-home placements seems to have occurred between 1977 and 1978, when there was a drop of more than 180 children in placement (-20.2 percent) from the previous year. In attempting to determine why such a significant decline in placements occured during this time, it was found that during the two years DYFS out-of-state placement practices had changed considerably.

The foremost reason for this resulted from pressure brought about, particularly by the Public Advocate's office, regarding the large number of children placed by the Division in out-of-state facilities. Historically, the Division had made use of out-of-state residential facilities for children, for whom they argued, no resources seemed to exist in New Jersey. In March 1976, 864 children were placed out-of-state. These placements constituted 38.6 percent of the total number of institutional placements used. Opponents to this practice argued that the state was not assuming its responsibility for its children who were in need of services by sending them to out-of-state

TABLE 4

Children from Rural Counties in Out-of-Home Placement

1972	1973	1974	1975	1976	1977	1978	Total	Percent Change
935	873	831	887	871	910	726	6,033	-22.4%

Source: Quarterly Review on Whereabouts of Children Under Division of Youth and Family Services Supervision.

facilities and not providing needed resources within the state itself. Additionally, children who were placed in facilities in states such as Florida, lost all access to their families and communities, and in fact, were penalized for their disability, handicapping condition or illness that supposedly required out-of-home care. However, arguments by Division officials contended that there were insufficient resources within the state for children requiring services particularly those requiring intensive treatment. Nonetheless, during the past two years the Division reduced its out-of-state placement practices considerably, thereby also reducing the overall number of children in institutional placement. In Table 5 (on the following page) we note the change in statewide placement practices.

While placements have increased from 1972 to 1978 (17.8 percent), we can see the most substantial increase between 1972 and 1975 (39.7 percent). The first decline in total number of placements appeared in 1976, but 1976 also reflected more children in out-of-state placements than any other year. From 1975 to 1978, the number of institutional placements has decreased by slightly over 15 percent, while the number of out-of-state placements decreased by about 22 percent. However, from 1976 to 1978 the decreased use of out-of-state placements has been most notable (38.9 percent).

It is difficult at this time to infer that the use of residential placements will continue to decline. One could surmise that while out-of-state placements will decrease, there will be an eventual increase in overall placements, as a result of new facilities developing within the state, both public and private.

Summary

Overall, local activity in rural counties regarding the processing of juveniles through the juvenile justice network has been on the upswing, even prior to the 1974 code changes. Cases handled in court, use of pre-dispositional care facilities (as well as their development) and correctional commitments have increased. The use of state-subsidized residential placements has decreased markedly; however, this has been largely due to other reasons not attached to the code changes.

It seems necessary to understand to what extent the code made no substantial impact on the manner in which children are processed through juvenile justice agencies in terms of some basic policy issues. First, we note that the code made no provisions for excluding certain children from the juvenile justice system altogether. Its major provision was to make some categorical distinction separate from that of delinquency; however, with the exception of preventing the placement or commitment of status offenders to institutions for delinquents, these children are still handled in a manner similar to delinquents.

Second, while there seems to be no reduction of children involved in juvenile justice agencies, the code has resulted in prohibiting the placement of status offenders in restrictive settings such as detention centers. We note the significant decrease of detention placements, even though there has not been any decrease in the use of pre-dispositional placements. This is related to the development of a particular issue not originally anticipated with the passage of the 1974 legislation. JINS shelters are many times used for reasons other than temporary placement for the supposed commitment of a status

TABLE 5

Children in Institutional Care By Year

	1972	1973	1974	1975	1976	1977	1978	Percent change
Total in institutions	1,721	1,842	2,081	2,405	2,238	2,178	2,028	+17.8
Number in out-of-state facilities	669	707	614	676	864	690	528	-21.1
Percent of all institutional placements	38.9	38.4	29.5	28.1	38.6	31.7	26.0	

Source: State of New Jersey, Department of Human Services, Division of Youth and Family Services, March Quarterly Reports of Children Under Supervision.

offense. The statute requires that a child only be placed in temporary shelter care if they are charged with an offense. However, DeJames and Dannefer noted:[4]

> Family dysfunction often creates situations where juveniles can not, or should not, live at home, either for brief or extended periods of time. In some of these situations, juveniles must be immediately placed outside of their homes. The only temporary alternative, given the lack of alternative resources, may be a JINS shelter, where juveniles must first be charged as "offenders" before they are admitted. This situation clearly increases the number of JINS complaints filed against juveniles. In some cases, it is quite apparent that the sequence of events involving the juvenile's misbehavior, the signing of the complaint, and the placement in custody is different for delinquents and JINS. In a typical delinquent situation, the juvenile commits an offense, is subsequently apprehended and a complaint signed, and then a decision is made regarding the need for secure custody in detention. Many JINS cases, however, result from a much different sequence of events: the decision to place the juvenile in a JINS shelter is sometimes made before the decision regarding the need for a complaint. Thus, the complaint merely becomes the vehicle for admission into the JINS shelter. This is why the proportion of JINS placed in temporary custody is two to three times higher than the comparable proportion of delinquents placed in detention.

Thus, after more than five years since the new code came into being, we now see a concern that there are children involved with New Jersey juvenile justice agencies, for no reasons other than there are reportedly no resources. In order for a child to get services, assuming he needs them, he has to become involved with a system that defines him as an offender, even though he has not committed any type of offense--even a status offense. This backhanded practice of providing resources seems to typify the archaic manner in which children are continuously labeled, penalized, and subjected to various means of social control for which they have no need.

Last, the impact of legislation such as the New Jersey JINS law is often times difficult to measure, especially when required changes in practices result in development of additional resources such as shelter facilities. The addition of resources many times results in marked increases of persons served, or identified to be "in need" of services, e.g. if one builds an institution there will be people to go into it. This seems to have been the case among this small sample of rural counties.

---

[4]Ibid., pp. xxxiii-xxxiv.

Part III

RURAL STRATEGIES FOR HELPING TROUBLED YOUTH

Introduction

At the heart of the "rural delinquency" problem is a basic need to gain an understanding of the special needs of rural youth and program strategies which can best meet these needs. Both our review of the literature and contacts with individuals/programs throughout the country have resulted in the identification of numerous attempts presently employed in various communities which take into consideration the unique problems of rural youth.

Stephen Dahl presents a descriptive analysis of the delinquent youth residing in a rural area. Certain factors contribute to the delinquent behavior and serve to further a youth's alienation from existing social systems. First, the youth is much more visible to other people than his/her urban counterpart--perceptions often become distorted and result in a youth being subjected to community hostility or harrassment.

Second, parents often lack an understanding of their child's behavior. This generally results in their inability to cope with their child's problems, thus producing considerable strain on family relations. Third, school systems in rural areas have difficulty in assisting children who continually fail, due to lack of resources and trained personnel. The labeling of "troublemakers" eventually forces children out of the school system. Dahl also gives concrete suggestions as to how social workers and other public agency workers can best provide services to troubled children and their families.

Forslund's study of adolescent self-reporting of drug use and delinquency patterns found that more male and female nonusers reported they'd never committed a delinquent act. On the other hand, a higher number of self-reported drug users also reported previous delinquent activity. His research infers there is a relationship between drug use and anti-social behavior. Also, drug users perceived greater problems in their relationships with their parents, had lower grades and dropped out of school more frequently than nonusers.

Kenneth Libertoff explores issues pertaining to runaways and how they are unique to rural areas. He suggests, with some detail, that there are six social networks in which runaway children fund themselves: police-legal, mental health, social welfare, self-help/youth advocacy, helping, peer-adult and no networks.

He also describes a model rural program in central Vermont that was developed as a result of the 1974 Runaway Youth Act. Its major emphasis is to provide a "network of supportive, helping families" who house and assist children.

Shepard discusses an important set of issues closely allied with juvenile justice: child abuse and protection in the rural setting. She places abuse within the context of socio-economic deprivation and relates it to basic problems of rural services delivery, e.g., isolation, transportation and inadequate housing. Also, she discusses the reality that parental stress and family crisis are difficult to prevent and treat in the rural environment since "scarce, formal resources concentrated in areas of dense population isolate rural family from essential services." She offers basic programmatic suggestions to deal with these problems which include: creative use of existing resources, outreach, community organization and better coordination of existing services.

Edmund Dimock presents the rationale behind the use of short-term group homes in rural areas. The presence of such a facility in a rural community serves various functions for troubled adolescents, in that it: (1) provides distance between emotionally destructive parents and their child; (2) decreases the need to run away; (3) breaks up a family's unhealthy communication system; (4) provides emotional distance; (5) removes pressure on parents; and (6) provides a structured environment. Most importantly, a nonrestrictive facility such a group home, serves as a much better alternative to existing juvenile justice agencies and removes some of the stigma normally associated with such programs.

Lawless examines the vocational problems of rural youth and how lack of such opportunities often results in disenchantment and delinquent behavior. He suggests that meaningful employment opportunities for rural adolescents can serve as a basic means to achieve autonomy and independence, self-esteem and responsibility. Additionally, he describes a youth-operated business in Topsfield, Massachusetts which is sponsored by the Tri-Town Council on Youth and Family Services, Inc.

Jankovic addresses issues which impede the implementation of progressive education in rural areas and how these issues impact children and their families. Identifying the rural school system as a primary point for early identification and intervention for troubled children, she discusses basic problems confronting school social workers and other educational personnel who attempt to advocate and protect interests of school children; professional isolation, community perceptions of professional roles and social/political realities common to each rural community. Also, she offers several suggestions as to how educational justice can be best assured within the rural setting.

CHAPTER VII

THE DELINQUENT YOUTH IN THE RURAL AREA

by Stephen Dahl

The Waushara (Wisconsin) County Department of Social Services provides services to those youth who come within the jurisdiction of the county Juvenile Court system. The majority of these cases are delinquency, in need of supervision, or dependency matters. The referrals are usually ordered by the Juvenile Court or are informally referred by the Waushara County Sheriff's Department. The agency provides services to youth with problems labeled as truancy, runaways, criminal behavior and drug and alcohol abuse. There are approximately 65 youths per year who are receiving services either from an agency social worker or the county Juvenile Court worker. This is approximately one-fifth of the total number of children who come in contact with the Sheriff's Department. In 1975 there was a total of approximately 300 children who came to the attention of the county Sheriff's Department and Juvenile Court. This is nearly seven percent of the county's total juvenile population.

The rural youth who enters Waushara County's Juvenile Court process typically is male and has experienced other problematic behavior within his social environment. His family is likely to describe the child as a difficult to control youth who spends an exaggerated amount of time with his peers. The child often has a school history of poor grades and attendance; he plans to drop out of school at age 16, if he hasn't already done so. The juvenile will usually have a difficult time objectively discussing "why" he participated in an unlawful incident or refused to attend school. The youth can, however, tell you a lot about himself by his indifference, distrust, and verbal complaint about his parents, teachers or other significant people within his surroundings.

The child can be described as alienated from many adults and peers. The degree of alienation will largely depend upon how supportive the child's social systems have been in the past. If a child has had a positive relationship with the significant people in his environment, he will likely continue to exhibit appropriate behavior and maintain a more positive attitude about himself. The delinquent youth generally has had less positive experiences within his environment. The family and school systems, typically, will grow more frustrated and intolerant towards a child's inappropriate behavior. This has a tendency to strengthen a child's resentment and alienation.

The delinquent youth who grows more alienated will also seem to be experiencing an "identity crisis." This is normal for most adolescents who are growing more independent from the adults in their life. The adolescent who has grown distrustful and feels rejected from his adult world will, however, have difficulty in completing this developmental task. He will likely compensate by seeking emotional support, acceptance and status from his peers. These peers are usually other adolescents who are experiencing similar problems at home and school. The child will largely over-identify with them and his relationships with peers become more important than the expectations of his family and school. The adolescent, for example, will want to continually be with his peers, and he won't care if he gets home at a reasonable hour in the evening. He may also skip classes more frequently with his schoolmates. It is likely that the youth will again seek refuge or support from his peers when his parents and school officials try to regain control of the situation.

The youth who is engulfed within this group process will probably maintain a feeling that it is "us against everyone else." This not only includes many adults in the youth's life, but other peers who are conforming to traditional expectations from their family and school. This juvenile, for example, will identify himself as separate from the "jocks" at school and adapt his own style of dress and probably participate in his group's own unique activities. This type of cohesiveness increases the likelihood that the youth will engage in more deviant behavior within his group. A delinquent act, for example, will give the youth an opportunity to gain more recognition or status within his group. This process is strongly operative within Waushara County, since most youths are accompanied by a companion in their offense. The majority of our referrals are typically group offenses, such as the possession of alcohol or marijuana, vandalism, theft or burglary and truancy.

The understanding of delinquent behavior is not just unique to the rural areas. There are, however, three factors which we believe are contributing to the occurrence of delinquent behavior in our area and aggravating the youth's alienation and identity crisis. The first factor is that a youth in a rural town is much more visible to other people in comparision to an urban area. This greater visibility has a tendency to reinforce or strengthen people's perceptions towards a particular child or anyone else. People have more opportunities to think about another person, as they come in indirect or direct contact with each other more often. They will, in other words, (1) be in closer proximity to one another and therefore see each other more often; and (2) have a greater access to information about each other through the informal communication network of a rural town. A major aspect of this is that it often leads to many distorted perceptions of other people since most people are only exposed to limited information. The child who develops problems within school or with the law, or has had a family with a history of problems, is likely to find himself labeled as a troublemaker, a freak, undeserving or different. Many townspeople, for example, will know if a child was contacted by a police official or skipped out of school. The child is certainly very visible when he is standing around on main street with his friends who have long hair and dirty clothes. These things are likely to reinforce people's negative perceptions towards a particular youth. A youth can easily become conscious of these attitudes by the indifference or hostility others might project. The youth, for example, could be unjustly harassed by the town policeman, be unfairly denied a job or told not to return to a store by the merchant. The youth is very helpless in defending himself against this labeling process. He has no power or credibility to challenge those who have affixed a stigmatizing label on him.[1]

The second factor which increases the problems of delinquent youth in the rural area is that the familial system lacks the ability to cope with the problems of these youths. The family has had a limited understanding of the child's behavior, and therefore has had a tendency to react intolerantly and authoritatively towards these problems. The parents will initially try to resolve their child's truancy problem delinquent behavior or any normal

---

[1]Robert W. Winslow, Juvenile Delinquency in a Free Society 2nd Edition, 1968, p. 95.

developmental problem, but will lack the ability to consistently control or stay on top of the situation. They generally lack the time, energy and knowledge, largely because they are burdened with other problems which typically have a higher incidence in rural areas, such as alcoholism, inadequate education, unemployment, divorce and marital problems and low incomes. A parent, for example, will be preoccupied with personal problems and struggling to make ends meet. The child's problem merely represents another burden or crisis. These parents traditionally may try to resolve the problem by taking something away from the child or by threatening to have them sent away to the boys' home or a state institution. They may also request that their son not associate with a best friend whom they feel is a bad influence. The child resents such a parental response because the friend is of primary importance to him. The parents may also respond in a defensive or over-protective manner when a school official or law official identifies a problem with the youth. They view the intervention from a social worker, teacher, policeman or the court as very threatening. They feel they are being blamed for their child's behavior and to them it can only represent another failure. The results are: (1) the parents are often erratic or inconsistent in responding to their child's developmental needs and/or trying to impose appropriate sanctions for their child's behavior--once the initial crisis subsides for the child, the parents will again turn to their own problems; and (2) the parents will lack the willingness to cooperate with the school or a social agency; they will likely go through the motions of the agency's case plan, and subtly sabotage change efforts.

The third factor which appears to contribute to delinquency is the rural school's response toward these youth and their problems. They are often unable to deal with school failure which develops in the early elementary grades. It is typical to examine the school record of a delinquent youth and discover that he has been failing and has had a poor attendance record since fourth grade. The problem is that the delinquent youth doesn't fit in a special educational program, though he needs more than a regular classroom to motivate him. The school board members don't appear ready to finance an alternative education program like those in many larger cities. The reasons seem to be: (1) the rural school doesn't have as many students who could benefit from an alternative education program as there are in urban areas; and (2) school board members presently don't appear willing to finance a program for the long-haired, goof-off or undeserving kid. It further seems that the schools are having a difficult time knowing how to confront the problems. They are unsure of how much responsibility they have to resolve failures in school. They typically understand school failure as inherently resulting from the family. This is true, particularly with low income families. The problem is that schools often neglect to understand how they are contributing to the situation.

The rural school system, like urban schools, shows a definite pattern of responses toward a student's acting out behavior, incomplete assignments and poor attendance. The schools in our area deal with these problems by imposing an increasing amount of restrictive measures on a student. A principal, for example, will detain a student after school for skipping a class or smoking a cigarette in the hallway. The youth will probably abide by the principal's disciplinary actions for a short time, but will soon develop a feeling that it is not worth it anymore. The youth who has limited success will soon come to the realization that there is no payoff in following the school rules and guidelines. The student who is repeatedly blamed for his negative behavior and who rebels against the school's sanctions will make himself more visible to the principal, the teachers and the school secretaries. An increasing number of complaints will probably surface toward this student and, in actuality, the complaints will likely become more petty and insignificant. The youth will be blamed more often for things he didn't do because of his past association with other problems. It becomes a very demeaning process for the juvenile and he will have greater difficulty in concentrating on normal school activities. The youth may withdraw or react very defensively towards each additional accusation. He will probably begin to demonstrate a poorer attitude in his classes and frequently skip his classes or not show up for school. The labeling process will eventually lock the youth out of the system and he will have no other alternative than to drop out of school.

A social worker who delivers services to the rural delinquent youth finds that "you are your own best resource." One essential reason is that the social worker holds the only position within the county that deals directly with the delinquent youth. This imposes a considerable amount of power and responsibility with one person. The way Waushara County's Juvenile Court functions, for example, increases the social worker's responsibility in making appropriate decisions for the lives of these children. The court can be described as participating in a rather passive manner throughout the juvenile court process. The judge, for example, will consistently follow the social worker's recommendations regarding the disposition of a child alleged to be delinquent, "in need of supervision" or dependent. The social worker also has a considerable amount of autonomy in deciding when to terminate or continue with a case. Furthermore, the county's district attorney has limited time to devote to local juvenile court matters, partially because the position is only half-time. The social worker, for example, will wait from one to three months before this office completes a juvenile court petition. A result is a limited degree of checks and balances within this court process. The court's disposition, for example, shouldn't be based solely on one worker's perspective or recommendations. The social worker who works within such a system is left in a rather vulnerable and liable position. It is therefore very important for the worker to safeguard against such a position by careful documentation of the court's investigations.

Another important aspect, is the stigma the community maintains towards the role of the social worker. The worker, for example, will generally receive limited cooperation from the community because the delinquent and his family will usually maintain a low status and influence within the community. It seems that people will dismiss any responsibility for a youth once he is placed under juvenile court supervision. This is significant because if the social agency doesn't support a child's development or pursue a particular case, it is likely that no one else will either.

An important facet of "you are your own best resource" is that there are a limited amount of other resources to bear upon these problems. One major deficiency is that the rural community has limited programs or opportunities for a youth to use his time in a constructive and meaningful manner. The youth has no recreational program to attend in the evenings and after school. The youth could attend the school's traditional activities and functions, except the delinquent youth is typically resistant to the school's rules and supervision at these activities. The lack of employment opportunities for local youth is further limited. There is seasonal work with local farmers or a few openings with the youth work experience program, but generally there aren't many opportunities for steady, full-time or part-time employment. The amount of a youth's idle time certainly seems to have a bearing on the fact that many referrals are for drinking alcohol or smoking marijuana. It also contributes to the problems of the delinquent youth who drops out of school and is not able to find employment.

Another gap in local resources is the social agency that is unable to find temporary placement for a child who has run away from home or is in need of a rest or "out" period away from home. The agency traditionally has placed a child in detention or the county jail or has sent the child back home to his parents. The first option is usually unnecessary and inappropriate for the child who is in need of supportive environment, rather than the isolation of the county jail. In 1975 there were 29 children who were placed in detention and of this number, 18 or 62 percent could have benefited from an alternative placement. In the latter incident, when the child is sent back home, it seems that we are sending the child into a revolving door. In 1975 it was estimated that 82 children or 35 percent of a total of 318 children who came in contact with the agency and the sheriff's department could have benefited from an alternative placement. In the past, a child occasionally was placed in a foster home. These placements are rare since many foster parents do not want the adolescent youth in their homes and also because the agency is hesitant to make such a placement since they usually know very little about the youth. When all else fails, it is not atypical for members of the social work staff to take the youth into their own homes. In the near future, the agency hopes to be better able to deal with these situations. Waushara County Department of Social Services is in the process of securing funds to develop a temporary placement or a sheltered home facility. The significant aspect of this project is that it is a joint venture with two other adjacent counties. This joint effort is necessary to be able to demonstrate a large enough need and to be able to financially support such a project.

The Department of Social Service's traditional casework approach to the delinquent youth and the family is basically the most well-developed resource or method for handling these problems. Still, this approach is often inadequate in bringing about significant change within the youth's present surroundings. This inadequacy is evident by the recidivism of those juveniles who come in contact with law officials and the juvenile court, and also by the high number of youths who are committed to state institutions. In the latter instances, there were 11 youths in 1974 from Waushara County who served in correctional institutions. This was .3 percent of the county's juvenile population. Waushara County ranked 10.5 within the state on a high to low scale. In 1975 there were nine youths that served in a state correctional institution.

In approaching these problems as a social worker, one has a tendency to become overwhelmed by the continual struggle of providing resources, the communities' intolerance to clients and by the degree of problems within the social system. A key point to overcome these helpless feelings is to recognize that the social worker's major responsibility is to identify each problem within the context of the total situation and to provide the necessary feedback to these social systems so they understand how they are contributing to the problem. The agency is essentially shifting the responsibility to the youth and his surroundings. The worker's objective is to help these social systems develop new approaches or coping strength, in responding to these problems. There are still going to be many drawbacks or little success on a case-by-case basis. The focus is, however, to help people react to the causes of their problems, not the traditional reaction to the <u>symptoms</u> of the problems.

In working with alienated youth within his family, there is a need to be an advocate in bringing out the youth's feelings. The parents need to understand the normal developmental stages of their child and recognize that their child is still a good person, despite bad behavior. The worker's objective is at least to reduce the parents' intolerant feelings towards their child and, if possible, to redevelop a trusting relationship between them. An example of this process can be demonstrated when a child is found in possession of marijuana. The parents' reaction has a tendency to create more problems than does the child's actual drug use. The parents will usually hold many fallacies about the use of marijuana. It becomes necessary to provide the family with a rather instructive role in discussing the physical and psychological effects of the drug. The worker should attempt to bring out the child's attitude about the use of the drug as well as the reasons that led up to the actual drug use. In this particular example, the youth may even continue to smoke pot, but the worker could have desensitized the parents, so they may respond to their child in a nonthreatening way.

Parents who erratically discipline their child need some education in parenting techniques. They must recognize that they cannot expect their child to change unless they respond appropriately towards him. The worker can suggest appropriate consequences for the youth's negative behavior. This is usually needed because in the past the youth has not responded to the parents' threats which in most cases have been unreasonable or unenforceable. In view of parental inconsistency, it is necessary for the worker to follow up with the parents to insure that they do not lose sight of their responsibility. The implementation of a behavior management program for the parents and their child can often be an effective method of dealing with these issues.

In intervening within many families, the worker will often find it impractical to maintain the focus solely on the child's problem. It is likely another child in the family will be experiencing other problems or the parents will have their own personal problems which have a bearing upon the children. The worker will likely have to expand the scope of the intervention to other members of the family because: (1) it is impractical to refer each case to the local mental health clinic in a rural area; and (2) the worker is the most accessible to the problems. The mother and father of a client, for example, are experiencing serious problems in their marriage. The worker was unsuccessful in providing linkage to the county's marriage counselor because the husband refused to cooperate or face his marriage problems. The worker may continue to stay involved with this problem by helping the mother cope with the situation.

The Waushara County Department of Social Services has traditionally limited intervention with the county's local schools. The agency needs to improve its casework efforts with local schools as well as pursue more formal cooperation with these schools on a class action basis. This means the agency needs to maintain ongoing communication with the principal and teachers about the client's progress and further develop a method whereby personnel from the county's school system, social agency, mental health agency and law enforcement agency can exchange ideas about these problems. In intervening on a casework basis with local schools, the worker most often is in an advocate role. This is demonstrated by the following objectives that a worker can become involved with.

1. There is a definite need to arrange an opportunity for the youth to express his feelings about a particular problem situation. For example, if a youth, has been in past trouble at school he will have limited opportunities to tell his side of the story.

2. The worker can suggest less authoritative methods of discipline for a client's negative behavior. The objective is to maintain the youth's respect for the school's authority and to hold the youth within the system rather than locking him out. A youth who repeatedly disrupts a teacher's classroom could typically be suspended after repeated warnings. It might be more appropriate, however, for the school to remove the youth from the particular class instead of giving him a three-day vacation.

3. A network of communication needs to be established and pursued by the worker so that both the school and social agency are not operating within a vacuum. The purpose is to provide each with enough information to reduce the likelihood that any distorted perceptions towards a particular youth will develop. This may be accomplished by a worker-teacher conference or by staffing the case with the youth's teachers, the counselor or other significant people within the school. These conferences could also provide these people with an opportunity to vent any hostile feelings, therefore lessening the chance they would be directed to the student.

4. The worker needs to assure that the client is receiving an educational program appropriate for his psychological and physical condition. This could mean that the worker provides the client with access to the school psychologist for evaluation. A further example is the worker could intervene to assure that a pregnant high school girl has been given the options of homebound instruction or remaining in school.

5. The last objective is to assure that the school has not neglected to refer a truancy problem or any other matter that should appropriately be handled within the jurisdiction of the juvenile court. In some instances a local school will neglect to refer a truancy problem to the court because the student is almost old enough to quit. The school may also neglect to refer a truancy problem until the latter part of the school year when it should have been referred after it first developed in the beginning of the year. In another instance, the school should definitively refer the case when the child's parents significantly contribute to their child's truancy problem. This is particularly necessary for a younger child who is being kept away from school because of the social needs of the mother.

There is a definite need for local county officials to meet and discuss broader issues related to troubled youth. The group should have representation from all professionals in the community who are directly or indirectly involved with these problems. An initial group goal is to develop an objective understanding of these problems and determine what they want to do about them. Professional members from our schools, social agencies and the sheriff's department began to discuss common problems during the 1975-76 school year. The ad hoc group limited progress throughout last year largely because it was unable to clarify the group's focus.

In the future the group could address some of the following tasks: The need to identify and document problem areas which need attention--this, for example, could mean documenting the school's dropout rate or detecting those children who are beginning to fail in the elementary grades; the need to understand how local agencies and schools respond to these problems and how professionals can deal more effectively with these problems--this could mean studying the school's pattern of responses in disciplining or motivating these youths. The development of a model for the interrelationships of schools and social agencies could also be beneficial in clarifying when it is necessary to refer a case to juvenile court or whether a social worker should intervene with the client's school situation.

In conclusion, a worker must be careful not to over-identify with the needs and feelings of the rural delinquent youth. The youth who is perpetually complaining about how everyone is against him often pushes the worker into a rather overprotective role. The worker can safeguard against such a problem by working within the youth's total surroundings. In essence, the social worker must help others react to the causes of a child's delinquent behavior rather than the symptoms.

CHAPTER VIII

DRUG USE AND DELINQUENT BEHAVIOR OF SMALL TOWN AND RURAL YOUTH

by Morris A. Forslund

There are numerous references in the criminological literature to the relationship between drug use and other forms of criminal behavior. For example, Swezey has recently published data on drug-crime relationships for adults[1] and it is frequently pointed out that especially in metropolitan areas many female addicts turn to prostitution while many male addicts engage in one or another type of property crime to obtain money to purchase drugs. With respect to juveniles, however, there are few references in the literature to the relationship between drug use and other types of delinquency. Among these, Cloward and Ohlin have noted that members of "retreatist" delinquent subcultures have often been first involved in "conflict" or "criminal" subcultures, and successful "cats" have "hustles" which may involve such illegal activities as stealing, petty con games or pimping.[2] But they provide no empirical data concerning the relationship between drug use and specific other types of delinquent behavior, and their conclusions refer primarily to metropolitan area subcultural delinquency. Virtually nothing is known about the relationship between drug use and other forms of delinquency among small town and rural area youth.

The Present Study

The findings presented here are based on responses to a self-report type questionnaire concerning delinquent acts which was administered to ninth through twelfth grade students at two high schools in Fremont County, Wyoming in May of 1972. One high school is located in a town of approximately 8,000 population and the other is located in a rural area. Thus the backgrounds of the students studied are generally small town and rural ranching-farming in nature. The total sample consists of 456 males and 391 females. No significant differences were found in drug use patterns between students attending the two high schools.

For purposes of this study a drug user is defined as any student who indicated that he or she had used marijuana or any other drug for "kicks" or pleasure during the year preceding the administration of the questionnaire. Of the males in the sample, 79.8 percent had used neither marijuana nor other drugs "during the past year," 1.1 percent had used other drugs but not marijuana, 12.5 percent had used marijuana but not other drugs, and 6.6 percent had used both marijuana and other drugs. Of the females, 81.8 percent had used neither marijuana nor other drugs "during the past year," 2.3 percent had used other drugs but not marijuana, 7.7 percent had used marijuana but not other drugs, and 9.0 percent had used both marijuana and other drugs.

---

[1] R.W. Swezey, Estimating Drug-Crime Relationships, The International Journal of the Addictions, 8, pp. 701-721, 1973.
[2] R.A. Cloward and L.E. Ohlin, Delinquency and Opportunity: A Theory of Delinquent Gangs, Free Press, New York, 1960.

Of those who had smoked marijuana "during the past year," 47.2 percent of the males and 50.0 percent of the females had done so only once or twice, while 27.6 percent of the males and 25.0 percent of the females had smoked marijuana on ten or more occasions. Of those who had used other drugs, 42.9 percent of the males and 44.2 percent of the females had done so only once or twice "during the past year," while 25.7 percent of the males and 18.6 percent of the females had used other drugs on ten or more occasions.

The majority of the students used marijuana or other drugs in the company of one or more friends. Only 16.7 percent of the males and 6.9 percent of the females indicated that they usually used marijuana or other drugs alone.

Drug Use and Delinquency

Table 1 (on the following page) represents data concerning the relationships between drug use and 26 other forms of delinquent behavior for the male students in the sample studied. Inspection of these data reveals that with respect to all 26 types of delinquent acts a higher percentage of nonusers than users stated that they had never committed these acts "during the past year." At the other extreme, with regard to all of the 26 acts a higher percentage of users than nonusers stated that they had committed these acts three or more times "during the past year." For 23 of the 26 types of delinquent acts the difference between users and nonusers with regard to frequency of commission is statistically significant.

Table 2 (on page 93) presents data concerning the relationship between drug use and the same 26 types of delinquent acts for the female students in the sample. Examination of these data shows that in every case a higher percentage of nonusers than users indicated that they had never committed these acts "during the past year." And, in 25 of the 26 cases a higher percentage of users than nonusers stated that they had committed the act three or more times during that period. For 15 of the 26 types of delinquent acts the difference between users and nonusers in the frequency of commission of the act is statistically significant.

The students were also asked: "Have you ever been found guilty of a traffic offense other than a parking violation?" and "Have you ever been found guilty of an offense other than a traffic violation?" Among males, a significantly higher percentage of users (30.4%) than nonusers (13.1%) indicated that they had been found guilty of a traffic offense other than a parking violation (X^2 = 14.56, 1df, $p<.001$). There is, however, virtually no difference in the percentages of female users (5.5%) and nonusers (5.1%) who have been convicted of such an offense. With respect to convictions for offenses other than traffic violations, there is a significant difference between users and nonusers for both males and females; male users, 34.8 percent--male nonusers, 14.8 percent (X^2 = 17.67, 1df, $p<.001$); female users, 20.5 percent--female nonusers, 6.0 percent (X^2 = 13.94, 1df, $p<.001$). Thus, drug users both report a higher incidence of involvement in most forms of delinquent behavior and a higher percentage of users than nonusers have been convicted of such offenses.

TABLE 1

The Relationship Between Drug Use and Frequency of Commission of Other Types of Delinquent Acts Among Male High School Students

Delinquent Act	User			Nonuser			
	% Never	% 1-2	% 3+	% Never	% 1-2	% 3+	P <
Truancy	28.3	26.1	45.6	62.4	23.1	14.5	.001
Skipped School	27.2	19.6	53.3	52.1	24.3	23.6	.001
Disobeyed teacher, school official	11.0	37.4	51.6	36.6	33.2	30.2	.001
Signed name to school excuse	64.1	17.4	18.5	86.0	9.5	4.5	.001
Disobeyed parents	5.5	18.7	75.3	10.6	32.4	57.0	.01
Defied parents to their face	37.0	31.5	31.5	61.8	25.6	12.5	.001
Ran away from home	73.9	18.5	7.6	91.6	6.7	1.7	.001
Said mean things to get even	14.1	27.2	58.7	19.9	34.6	45.4	
Made anonymous phone calls	55.4	15.2	29.3	68.4	14.4	17.2	.05
Trespassed	8.9	23.3	67.8	26.8	16.7	56.5	.01
Let air out of tires	50.0	21.7	28.3	67.1	21.4	11.4	.001
Marked on desk, wall, etc.	15.4	26.4	58.2	24.1	31.3	44.6	
Thrown eggs, garbage, etc.	39.6	26.4	34.1	61.2	16.6	22.2	.001
Broke windows	53.8	26.4	19.8	69.6	22.0	8.4	.01
Broke down clothesline, etc.	64.8	18.7	16.5	75.8	19.4	4.7	.001
Put paint on something	62.0	21.7	16.3	73.1	18.9	8.1	.05
Broke street light	63.0	16.3	20.7	76.5	16.1	7.5	.001
Taken things from desks, etc. at school	63.0	21.7	15.2	77.0	14.8	8.1	.02
Taken things worth under $2	39.1	28.3	32.6	58.3	26.3	15.4	.001
Taken things worth $2-$50	59.8	22.8	17.4	89.6	7.6	2.8	.001
Taken things worth over $50	80.4	10.9	8.7	96.9	1.7	1.4	.001
Taken car without owner's permission	76.1	16.3	7.6	88.0	8.7	3.4	.02
Drove car without license	33.0	23.1	44.0	34.5	26.1	39.5	
Fought--hit or wrestled	27.2	26.1	46.7	32.9	29.0	38.2	.05
Beat up someone	37.0	26.1	37.0	59.6	24.5	15.9	.001
Drank, parents absent	3.4	5.7	90.9	11.8	19.3	69.0	.001

TABLE 2

The Relationship Between Drug Use and Frequency of Commission of Other Types of Delinquent Acts Among Female High School Students

Delinquent Act	User			Nonuser			
	% Never	% 1-2	% 3+	% Never	% 1-2	% 3+	P <
Truancy	47.3	29.8	23.1	67.8	24.8	7.4	.01
Skipped school	27.0	29.8	43.3	56.1	25.4	18.5	.001
Disobeyed teacher, school official	19.2	35.6	45.2	40.5	39.2	20.3	.001
Signed name to school excuse	53.4	31.5	15.1	80.2	14.7	5.1	.001
Disobeyed parents	1.4	15.1	83.6	7.3	31.0	61.7	.01
Defied parents to their face	40.3	29.2	30.6	57.1	28.9	14.0	.01
Ran away from home	67.1	26.0	6.8	88.2	9.2	2.5	.001
Said mean things to get even	8.2	38.4	53.4	12.3	41.8	45.9	
Made anonymous phone calls	53.4	17.8	28.8	61.4	19.0	19.6	
Trespassed	12.3	31.5	56.2	24.8	32.7	42.5	.05
Let air out of tires	75.3	19.2	5.5	82.3	12.3	5.4	
Marked on desk, wall, etc.	11.0	34.2	54.8	17.1	38.3	44.6	
Thrown eggs, garbage, etc.	78.1	9.6	12.3	82.6	10.1	7.3	
Broke windows	89.0	9.6	1.4	92.7	6.3	0.9	
Broke down clothesline, etc.	76.7	17.8	5.5	89.5	8.6	1.9	.02
Put paint on something	69.9	24.7	5.5	81.3	15.8	2.8	
Broke street light	93.2	4.1	2.7	94.0	4.4	1.6	
Taken things from desks, etc. at school	82.2	13.7	4.1	91.1	7.0	1.9	
Taken things worth under $2	46.6	26.0	27.4	69.6	21.2	9.3	.001
Taken things worth $2-$50	75.3	17.8	6.8	91.4	5.8	2.9	.001
Taken things over $50	93.2	4.1	2.7	98.4	1.3	0.3	.05
Taken car without permission	80.8	17.8	1.4	90.1	7.3	2.5	.02
Drove car without license	32.9	23.3	43.8	44.4	20.3	35.4	
Fought--hit or wrestled	46.6	21.9	31.5	56.3	25.6	18.0	
Beat up someone	69.9	16.4	13.7	83.2	11.7	5.1	.02
Drank, parents absent	1.4	5.4	93.3	13.8	21.7	64.5	.001

Summary and Conclusion

These data demonstrate that there is a significant relationship between drug use and involvement in many other forms of delinquent behavior for both male and female adolescents. This relationship does, though, appear to be somewhat stronger for male than female high school students. Thus there is a strong tendency for youth, and particularly male youth, who use drugs to be involved in a variety of other types of anti-social conduct ranging from juvenile status offenses to felonies. Detailed examination of the data (not presented here because of space considerations and because of the small number of heavy drug users in the sample) also indicates a direct relationship between extent of involvement in drug use and frequency of commission of delinquent acts.

The data presented in Tables 1 and 2 in conjunction with other information obtained in this study also lead to the conclusion that drug users tend to have poorer relationships with both their parents and the school than is the case with regard to nonusers. In addition to the data already presented concerning truancy, skipping school, disobeying school officials or teachers, signing names to school excuses, disobeying parents, running away from home and taking things from desks or lockers at school, the following significant differences ($p<.05$) relevant to the relationships with parents and the school were found: both male and female drug users tend to perceive that they get along less well with both their father and their mother than is the case with nonusers; both male and female drug users tend to feel that they can discuss fewer problems with their parents than do nonusers; especially among females, nonusers tend to receive higher grades in school than users; among both males and females a higher percentage of nonusers than users definitely plan to graduate from high school; particularly among females, a higher percentage of nonusers plan to attend college; among both males and females a higher proportion of users than nonusers have dropped out of school; particularly among females, a higher percentage of users than nonusers feel that their classes are dull and boring.

There is, then, a strong tendency for youth who use drugs to be involved in a variety of other types of anti-social conduct and to have poorer relationships with both parents and schools than nonusers. The data do not, however, permit inferences with respect to the answers to other important questions. Does drug use tend to lead to a greater involvement in other forms of delinquency? Or, is engagement in other forms of delinquency conducive to drug use? Or, is there some common "cause" that underlies both drug use and engagement in a variety of other forms of delinquent? As noted above, Cloward and Ohlin contend that members of "retreatist" subcultures have often been first involved in "conflict" or "criminal" subcultures [2]. From his research in Chicago, Korbrin concluded that, "Persons who become heroin users were found to have engaged in delinquency in a group-supported and habitual form either prior to their use of drugs or simultaneously with their developing interest in drugs."[3] And the Board of Corrections, State of California tenatively concluded from a study of drug addicts in that state, "...that the use of drugs follows criminal activity and criminal

---

[3]S. Korbrin, Drug Addiction Among Young Persons in Chicago, Illinois Institute for Juvenile Research, Chicago, p. 6, 1953.

association rather than the other way around, which is often thought to be the case."[4] Perhaps involvement in other forms of delinquent behavior tends to precede drug use among small town and rural youth, too; this is an issue that can be resolved only through further research. But, if this is the case it seems likely that the probability of illegal drug use can be reduced by successful delinquency prevention programs.

---

[4]Board of Corrections, State of California, Narcotics in California, p. 9, 1959.

CHAPTER IX

THE RUNAWAY YOUTH ISSUE: IMPLICATIONS FOR RURAL COMMUNITIES

by Kenneth Libertoff

The central purpose of this chapter is to provide a clearer, more accurate perspective on understanding the runaway youth issue. Although this problem has been identified as an urban phenomenon (in no small way a reflection of the well publicized "flower years" of the 1960's), there is little doubt that many rural adolescents are runaways. Recent national trends have indicated that runaway children are no longer heading for urban centers, but choose instead to stay much closer to home. Since the United States Subcommittee on Juvenile Delinquency has estimated that the annual number of runaway children may be as high as one million, this issue should be of great interest and concern to professionals in the human services field.

Because workers in rural communities have had little or no experience with meeting the needs of runaway children, this paper will also describe the development of one innovative model for working with these youths in a country setting. This program, aptly named "Country Roads," is now being implemented by the Washington County Youth Service Bureau in central Vermont.

An Overview

Although some experts believe that "running away" is of recent vintage, runaway children were among the earliest immigrants to the eastern shores of this nation. There is little doubt that the runaway child was familiar in the settlement and development of the original thirteen colonies. Running away to America and more significantly, running away while in America, has traditionally grown out of a mixture of youthful expectations and despair over current life circumstances.

Running away to this country was part of the founding of this nation. There is much evidence to suggest that the runaway child in America has played an important role in the growth and development of this country. There are numerous accounts of many young and daring teenagers who left home in search of a better life. Not surprisingly, some of these youths were to become America's greatest heroes. Benjamin Franklin offers an excellent example of how a spirited nature, a desire for travel and the need to assert personal independence led to an important runaway experience. Of course, running away was not confined to urban locations or more populated sections of the country. The history of rural America is filled with runaway episodes. The frontier was explored and settled by youths like Davy Crockett who ran away from his frontier Tennessee home at age 13 in order to escape a harsh father and travel in the western wilderness.

Over the years, many public officials and private citizens have expressed bewilderment over the fluctuating but continuous occurrence of this behavior. Yet a careful analysis of historical facts establishes the fact that periods of social change and stress have always increased the incidence rate of runaway behavior. This has been true during every American war, during periods of great economic turmoil and during times of cultural or social exploration.

The counter-culture youth movement of the 1960's is probably the best example of the latter variable. Running away to Harvard Square in Cambridge, Greenwich Village in New York and Haight-Ashbury in San Francisco became a publicized "happening." Many and perhaps even a majority of these youths were from comfortable middle- and upper-class families. When the runaway youth issue reached "middle America," often through the pages of Life, Time and Newsweek magazines, it became an issue of considerable attention and concern. The creation of the first "runaway houses" in the late 1960's and the passage of the Runaway Youth Act of 1974 are but two indicators of this keen interest.

The Literature

There appear to be few issues of current interest and importance, not to mention historical persistence, that have such a sparse and contradictory body of literature. There are three pronounced viewpoints throughout the literature. The first significant opinion is that running away is evidence of individual psychopathology. This segment of the literature most often defines the runaway child as disturbed, impulsive, disorganized and/or delinquent.[1] A second perception, while not necessarily refuting the former position, ascribes situational external forces such as family or school pressure as causative (or contributing) factors responsible for such behavior.[2] A third perhaps more contemporary theoretical assumption is that running away may be a natural outgrowth of certain predictable societal forces and may represent for some adolescents a healthy self-actualizing and growth-producing activity.[3]

There has been and continues to be a propensity to overlook several important variables that have affected, if not actually defined, the nature and scope of knowledge about runaway youth. While it is always beneficial to be concerned with organizing and synthesizing what is known about a subject, it may be just as necessary to identify and analyze that which is unknown or that which has not yet been investigated. These deficiencies or gaps in knowledge can also be instructive in the process of forming a framework for understanding the broader dimensions of the runaway phenomenon. There is reason to believe that the existing body of literature is more reflective and informative about the social networks that have interacted with this population of young people (as well as the professional training and field setting of the researcher) than about the actual subject under consideration.

Running away is an enigma for those who seek to investigate and study this behavior. Those who "leave home prematurely" are generally transient, often escaping from home or heading to some new or alternative destination. Because of many adverse legal sanctions, most young people on the run are

---

[1]R.S. Jenkins. "The Runaway Reaction." American Journal of Psychiatry, 128 (2), 1971: 168-173.

[2]G.E. Outland. "Determinants Involved in Boy Transiency." Journal of Educational Sociology, 11 (1938): 360-372.

[3]K. Libertoff. Perspectives on Runaway Youth. Boston: Massachusetts Committee on Children and Youth, 1976.

__________. Runaway Kids and Runaway Youth Programs: A Follow-Up Study. Boston: Project and Bridge and over Troubled Waters, 1976.

reluctant, or at least hesitant, to communicate or interact with traditional social settings. It is not surprising, therefore, that there is much uncertainty about the exact number of runaway adolescents from year to year.[4] Information about runaway behavior has come from investigations in urban, suburban and university communities. There has been little, if any, recognition of the runaway child in American rural communities.

Social Networks

Much of what is known about runaway children is a direct reflection of the kind of agency that over the years has maintained responsibility for this population. That is to say many runaway youths have been controlled, treated and/or served by a number of agencies which comprise several particular social networks. A careful reading of the literature suggests that knowledge about this phenomenon has been derived from four networks. These are identified as the police-legal network, the mental health network, the social welfare network, and the self-help youth-advocacy network. Two additional networks should also be categorized, although to this date there is almost no literature or information about either of them. They are designated as the helping peer-adult network, and the no network pattern of interaction.

Police-Legal Network

Young people under eighteen years of age who run away (that is, who leave home without parental permission) have been and generally still are considered lawbreakers in this country. The precise legal statutes in many states have been vague and unclear.[5] A warrant by a parent or the issuance of a stubborn or wayward child charge has frequently been sufficient grounds for the arrest and incarceration of a runaway child. Simply being away from home has made a young person vulnerable to legal sanctions and citizens who offer shelter to these youths are also in violation of the law. Despite recent efforts to de-criminalize these laws in many states young runaways are still adjudicated within the police-correctional network.[6] As in the past, juvenile courts, probation departments and reformatories still play a significant role in controlling these youths.

Mental Health Network

In recent decades, the mental health profession has become an important helping service as well as an influential treatment and controlling agent.[7]

---

[4]T. Brennan, S. Brewington and L. Walker. A Study of Issues Relating to Runaway Behavior. (Report prepared for the Office of Youth Development, Department of Health, Education and Welfare). Boulder, Colorado: Behavior Research and Evaluation Corporation, 1974.
[5]H.W. Beaser. The Legal Status of Runaway Children. Washington, D.C.: Educational Systems Corporation. (Prepared for the Department of Health, Education and Welfare), 1975.
[6]R.H. Andrews and A. Cohn. "The Unjustifiable Jurisdiction." The Yale Law Review, 83 (7): 1383-1409.
[7]I.I. Goldenberg. Build Me a Mountain: Youth, Poverty and the Creation of New Settings. Cambridge: MIT Press, 1971.

Psychiatrists and clinical psychologists have been involved in juvenile court clinics and child guidance centers. These clinicians have devoted much time to examining and diagnosing, and treating young people who have run away. Although there is considerable controversy and difference of opinion regarding the cause and meaning of runaway behavior, the American Psychiatric Association has officially categorized running away as a mental disorder.[8]

Social Welfare Network

Since the late nineteenth century when social reformers created special judicial procedures and correctional institutions for youthful offenders, a development that lead to the creation of the juvenile justice system, runaway children have been a concern to many social services agencies.[9] The Traveler's Aid Society, the Young Men's and Women's Catholic Association, settlement houses and various community emergency shelters are a few of the social welfare agencies that have worked with runaway youths since the turn of the century.

Self-Help Network

The self-help youth advocacy network is a product of the past decade.[10] Growing out of the anti-poverty efforts of the 1960's as well as the turbulent anti-war movement, this network represents a group of individuals who have, for the most part, rejected the professionalism of the clinician and the delinquency label of the police-correctional network. While lacking a precise ideology, most youth advocates view juveniles as powerless victims of an unjust and uncaring society. Therefore much effort is given to help young people gain control over their own lives. Workers in this network are frequently nonprofessionals who place emphasis on giving assistance to those young people who voluntarily request it. Because self-help workers, particularly those involved with runaway programs, have been primarily concerned with providing services, relatively little has been written about the interaction of runaway children and this network.

Peer-Adult Network

The first of the two less formal and recognizable networks is the helping peer-adult network. Many children who run away turn to their friends or peers for support and assistance. Runaway youths often communicate with a friend's parent, frequently a trusted and caring figure. In many cases, a helping peer or adult provide the first alternative shelter for a child who has departed from home. Helping peers and adults may also be total strangers. While for the most part this interaction is voluntary and supportive, some of

---

[8]Jenkins, op.cit.
[9]O. Nyquist. Juvenile Justice. London: MacMillan, 1960.
[10]J.S. Gordon. Working with Runaways and Their Families: How the SAJA Community Does It. Washington, D.C.: Center for the Studies of Child and Family Mental Health, National Institute of Mental Health, 1974.

these helping figures are neither benevolent or kind. Little is known about this network or its patterns of interaction.

No Network

The last network carries the ironic title of "no network." It covers the experience of those youths who leave home and do not interact with any of the aforementioned networks. In some context, these adolescents can be considered "successful runaways" because they leave home and manage independently without any formal network interaction. There is no literature and little recognition of these youths although their numbers may be considerable.

In order to further analyze the meaning of past research endeavors in the field, it is useful to examine in greater detail some of the interaction implications between those who have studied "runaway youth populations" and those who are among those populations. As previously mentioned, young people who run away are hard to locate. This simple fact poses special problems for those professionals who study these young people. Not surprisingly then, previous knowledge in the field is from settings, primarily those in the police-legal network and mental health network in which most runaways tend to be involuntarily captured, controlled and treated.

During the past 50 years, most of what has been written about the "runaway child" reflects research and investigation in the domain of the police-legal network, especially in detention homes, correctional institutions and court clinics. Since running away has been categorized as a law-breaking activity, the process of entering this network is a stigmatizing one and runaway adolescents are, at the very least, labeled as juvenile delinquents and troubled youths.

The mental health network, particularly the child guidance clinic, has historically been a major point of interaction between those who run away and those who study this behavior. Mental health professionals, most noticeably psychiatrists and psychologists, have been responsible for the diagnosis and treatment of these young people who are thought to be exhibiting deviant behavior patterns. These clinicians have exhibited a tendency to focus on the intrapsychic dynamics of the young person's behavior, frequently ignoring the psychosocial variables. Within the framework of their training, many of these professionals have often concluded that running away is a psychopathological disorder and mental illness.

Developing a Rural Program

In 1974, Congress approved and President Ford signed the Runaway Youth Act. This legislation marked the first federal response to the runaway youth issue. During the first several years of funding, urban, suburban and university communities received support for programs, most of which took the form of "runaway houses." These facilities frequently offered short-term residential care for from five to 15 youths. A staff of four to eight members, often recent college graduates, maintained these projects on a 24-hour, seven-day-a-week basis.

By early 1976, staff members of the Washington County Youth Service Bureau, a private, nonprofit organization in rural Vermont, were becoming increasingly aware and concerned about young people who were leaving home prematurely. On a regular basis, workers were being called upon to assist youthful runaways and transients. Some of these children were having great difficulty in getting along with their families; others were faced with physical or psychological abuse, school problems, unwanted pregnancies and extreme poverty. The Bureau, the county's only major youth serving agency, found that it was not able to adequately meet the special needs of these young people.

Staff members at the Bureau carefully considered several crucial variables in designing an appropriate runaway program for a rural environment. They were:

Assessment of Needs: Relative to urban communities and states, Vermont does not collect or maintain adequate data on youth needs and problems. The Youth Bureau therefore had to develop its own needs assessment plan.

Geographical Scope: The Bureau is responsible for all youth programs throughout a large rural county in central Vermont. The staff was eager to include all sections of this area in the model program.

Counseling Modalities: Because running away was viewed as a family dynamic, the Bureau was committed to working with teenagers and family members. This strategy called for some unique counseling approaches.

Community Acceptance: Vermonters pride themselves on being simple, independent and reserved people. A general resistance to change often makes the introduction of a new project quite difficult.

Financial Support: Vermont is a poor state with limited local resources. Yet the Bureau was committed to operating a quality program which included residential care, medical services and constant availablility.

"Country Roads"

After staff members considered and studied each of the previously mentioned issues, the Youth Bureau developed a runaway program called "Country Roads." This project has several unique attributes: it is the first rural program to be funded by the Office of Youth Development (HEW), which is administering the Runaway Youth Act, and it is also one of the few projects that is closely allied to the "helping peer-adult network," a network about which little is known.

The project revolves around creating a "network of supportive, helping families" within the central Vermont region. These families house and work with runaway teenagers, providing shelter, food and general support during a one-day to three-month period. The Bureau's runaway youth project coordinator provides constant training and guidance to these families and also develops a peer counseling program with runaway youths. The coordinator maintains the primary responsibility for working with the runaway child's family. While the primary aim of the project is to have young children return home, when that is not possible new alternatives are developed.

Country Roads has several other important goals. The first is to provide a safe, temporary, but supportive shelter for children away from home in a rural setting. The creation of alternative living situations is an important priority in rural environments. As a second expectation, Country Roads encourages the idea of family participation in local neighborhoods. These helping families provide a new community resource in rural areas where local provincialism, limited resources and geographical distances often inhibit the delivery of needed human services. A third and no less important goal is to encourage rural children and their families to seek assistance before problems reach the crisis stage. Obviously, prevention strategies are as important in country areas as they are in urban locations.

Summary

There is a great need to narrow the existing gap of knowledge and understanding of runaway children. Being neither a creation of the turbulent 1960's nor a minor passing fad, the issue of runaway adolescents in our society is now, and will continue to be, a major concern for years to come. Presently our society often labels runaway children as psychopathological or delinquent, or perhaps both. Yet there is much evidence to challenge and refute these assumptions.

A review of the history and literature about the runaway child in America reveals that young people from poor families have always viewed running away as a reasonable escape from a poverty-stricken home. For many adolescents, running away has been a response to an unhealthy family or work situation and at times it has been a problem-solving behavior. Since early colonial days, running away has been synonymous with seeking adventure, romance and fortune. Last but not least, running away has been an expression of independence, often marking the passage into adulthood. Periods of great social, economic, cultural and political change have always fostered runaway behavior and periods of war have also contributed to this syndrome.

Although running away has been viewed as an urban experience, there is growing evidence that rural communities are also in need of services for these youths. There is a concern, however, that rural human services workers will simply replicate urban programs as federal support becomes available. Programs like Country Roads in Vermont should help reinforce the belief that human service workers must develop appropriate models relevant to the special conditions and needs of rural environments.

BIBLIOGRAPHY

Aries, P. Centuries of Childhood. New York: Knopf, 1962.

Balser, B.H. "A Behavior Problem - Runaways." The Psychiatric Quarterly, 13 (1939): 539-557.

Becker, H.S. Outsiders. New York: A Free Press, 1963.

Chapman, C. America's Runaways. New York: Morrow and Company, 1976.

Erickson, E.H. The Challenge of Youth. New York: Doubleday, 1965.

Jacobs, C. "Planning an Adolescent Drug Treatment Project is a Rural Area: The Patchwork Approach to Program Development." (Paper presented at the First National Institute on Social Work in Rural Areas), Knoxville, Tennessee, July 15, 1976.

Kenniston, K. The Uncommitted. New York: Harcourt Brace and World, 1965.

Levine, M. and Levine, A. A Social History of Helping Services: Clinic, Court, School and Community. New York: Appleton-Century-Croft, 1970.

Ryan, W. Blaming the Victim. New York: Vintage Books, 1971.

Sarason, S.B., et al. Psychology in Community Settings: Clinical, Educational, Social, Vocational Aspects. New York: J. Wiley and Sons, 1966.

Walker, D.K. Runaway Youth: An Annotated Bibliography and Literature Review. Washington, D.C.: Office of the Assistant Secretary of Planning and Evaluation, Department of Health, Education and Welfare, 1975.

CHAPTER X

CHILD PROTECTION IN A RURAL SETTING

by Georgianna Shepard

Child protection in a rural setting poses a unique challenge. The beauty of the environment often masks the socioeconomic deprivation which may be present in rural as well as urban areas of the United States. Such deprivation contributes to parental stress and family crisis, which in turn, often precipitates child abuse. The treatment and prevention of child abuse in the rural environment is particularly difficult due to the absence of essential resources.

Representative of those rural areas with a high level of socioeconomic deprivation is Douglas County in the northwestern corner of Wisconsin. The county presents higher than statewide averages of divorce, unemployment, alcoholism and public assistance. According to five-year averages from 1968-72, Douglas County is tied for third place with urban Milwaukee County in the rate of divorce.[1] In relation to unemployment, Douglas County runs consistently above state and national levels. For example, in March 1976, the unemployment rate was 11.4 percent in Douglas County, compared with 7.0 percent for Wisconsin and 8.1 percent for the nation.[2] Even these harsh statistics do not fully portray the employment situation in rural Douglas County, where a large segment of the work force depends on seasonal lumber work or marginal farming.

Alcoholism is another striking problem. According to data compiled by the Douglas County Comprehensive Planning Board, the county's per capita incidence of alcoholism is among the highest in the nation.[3] The Wisconsin State Alcoholism Plan indicates that over 15 percent of the adult population is identified as alcoholics or alcohol abusers.[4] Finally, the public assistance recipient load provides just one indication that the county is an area of economic deprivation. In Wisconsin, the county ranks consistently at twelfth or thirteenth in public assistance recipient load, although there are approximately 21 Wisconsin counties larger in population.[5]

Other factors such as lack of adequate housing and insufficient opportunity for minority groups could also be cited, but the major point has been made. Socioeconomic deprivation is present in rural as well as urban communities. While definitive studies are yet to be made, it is obvious that the

---

[1]"Marriage and Divorce, Wisconsin, 1966-1970," Department of Health and Social Services, Division of Health, Bureau of Statistics, Section of Statistical Services. Table 22.

[2]Wisconsin State Employment Office, Superior, Wisconsin. Telephone conversation, April 1976.

[3]David Hon, Douglas County Comprehensive Planning Board, interview on June 14, 1976.

[4]Wisconsin State Alcoholism Plan for the Prevention, Treatment and Control of Alcohol Abuse and Alcoholism for the Fiscal Year 1975-76.

[5]John Barrett, Director, Douglas County Department of Social Services, memo, March 1976. His information was based on monthly statistics issued by the Division of Family Services on Public Assistance in Wisconsin.

presence of economic deprivation can do nothing to add to family stability and in fact is likely to contribute to parental stress.

Unlike many urban areas facing similar problems, rural areas are typically lacking in the resources necessary to combat them. Scarce or absent resources include public transportation, adequate recreational programs, basic health and social services, day care, adequate housing, vocational education, highways, museums, libraries and entertainment. Even though state and federal monies may be available to develop some of these resources, the typical county board may be unwilling to supplement these monies with county funds and will not apply for aid. Edward Buxton, in his article "Delivering Social Services in Rural Areas," indicated "...county boards do not see themselves as examining human needs and developing resources to meet these needs, but rather conceive of their role as one of holding back the director so that funds will not be over-expanded."[6]

Unfortunately, the matrix of rural socioeconomic deprivation combined with short resources does not tell the full story of factors contributing to parental stress. In addition, the few existing resources are concentrated in areas of relatively dense population, neglecting persons in rural areas. Douglas County exemplifies this concentration of resources. The population of 44,000+ persons is located in two principal sectors, the city of Superior and "the county," the area outside of Superior. The population of Superior is over 32,000 and the remaining 12,000 persons are dispersed over the rural countryside. Formal resources such as museums, recreation, vocational education, public transportation and libraries are usually centered in Superior. <u>All</u> formal health and social services, without exception, are located in Superior. Persons living on the perimeters of the county must drive distances up to 40 miles for service. The striking concentration of resources in areas of greater population points to the isolation of the rural family from formal services. The lack of any adequate public transportation makes the isolation especially dramatic. I have observed the same pattern as a resident of rural counties across the nation, including Berkshire County, Massachusetts and Antelope County, Nebraska. Seeing the rural setting from this perspective of scarce, inaccessible formal resources, it is possible to examine the effect on child abuse.

The thesis of this article is that the rural setting may contribute to child abuse in two ways:

1. The presence of socioeconomic deprivation contributes to parental stress and family crisis; child abuse may be the result.

2. Parental stress and family crisis are difficult to prevent and treat in the rural environment since scarce, formal resources concentrated in areas of dense population isolate the rural family from essential services.

---

[6]Edward Buxton, "Delivering Social Services in Rural Areas," <u>Public Welfare</u> Vol. 31, No. 1 (Winter 1973).

A review of the literature on child abuse gives substantial support to the fact that socioeconomic deprivation contributes to parental stress. Brandt F. Steele, M.D., comments:[7]

> [There is] increasing knowledge that child abuse and neglect occur among families from all socioeconomic levels, religious groups, races and nationalities. These facts should not be interpreted to deny the profound effect which social and economic deprivation, housing problems, unemployment, and subcultural and racial pressures have on the lives and behavior of the caretakers who abuse and neglect their children. Any stress can make life more difficult, and the ramifications of poverty can make anything worse than it would otherwise be.

More specifically, socioeconomic deprivation contributes to family crisis which is a precipitating, although not causative, factor in child abuse. Doctors Kempe and Helfer summarize three major pre-conditions which must exist before a child is physically injured by his parents or guardian. First, the parent or guardian must have the potential to abuse. Second, the child is seen as "different" by the parent or guardian. The third condition is summarized in this way:[8]

> Finally, there must be some form of crisis, or a series of crises, that sets the abusive act into motion. These can be minor or major crises--a washing machine breaking down, a lost job, a husband being drafted, no heat, no food, a mother-in-law's visit and the like. It would seem unlikely for the crisis to be the cause for the abuse, as some would like to believe; rather it is the precipitating factor.

Reviewing the examples of Doctors Kempe and Helfer, it is obvious that crises are exacerbated by socioeconomic deprivation. Certainly it would not be accurate to say that all crises are so caused or that all crises lead to child abuse, but one thing is certain: the problems of poverty and social alienation contribute to parental stress and family crisis.

So far, discussion of the socioeconomic deprivation role in child abuse has not differentiated the rural setting from the urban. The striking fact is merely that these problems are so prominent in the rural environment. It is when we look more deeply into the prevention and treatment of child abuse that we see unique aspects of the rural environment. As we noted earlier, the few available resources are inadequate and concentrated in areas of dense population. The troubled rural family is often effectively isolated from every form of help which might make their plight bearable. For example, a poverty-stricken couple with marital problems aggravated by alcoholism has no easy access to divorce counseling or treatment for chemical dependency. The couple has little relief from the care of children since there is usually no formal day care program in the county and certainly no crisis-centered child

---

[7]Brandt F. Steele, M.D., "Working with Abusive Parents from a Psychiatric Point of View," U.S. Department of Health, Education and Welfare, Publication No. (OHD) 75-70, page 3.
[8]C. Henry Kempe, M.D. and Ray E. Helfer, M.D., Helping the Battered Child and His Family, pages XIV-XV.

care center. Even the informal resources of relatives and friends may be located in the nearest town with no access by public transportation. Under these circumstances, parental stress rapidly mushrooms into a crisis when the mother becomes ill or the father loses his job. This crisis can become a precipitating factor in child abuse.

Thus the opportunity to prevent a family crisis is often lost. In addition, if child abuse does occur, treatment is hindered by the rural setting. The abuse may not come immediately, or even eventually, to the attention of the authorities due to the isolation of the family. If the child is brought to a distant hospital, the chances that this facility has a community-based child abuse treatment program, such as that described by Kempe and Helfer, are remote indeed.[9] Other remedial measures such as social casework, psychotherapy, vocational rehabilitation, chemical dependency programs and financial aid, are ordinarily located in the county seat and are not readily available to the family.

Considering these conditions, how are we to respond to the unique challenges of child abuse in the rural setting? Certainly there are no tried and tested answers. My suggestions concern the scarcity and availability of resources. First, realizing the scarcity of resources, each agency needs to plan its priorities with careful study of need. Once the existence of child neglect and abuse is documented, there is hope the community will make child protection a priority. Second, scare resources make it essential that agencies use all their resources and use them with imagination. For example, are para-professionals, such as homemakers and outreach workers, fully utilized in diagnosing and treating child abuse and neglect? Are volunteers working with neglectful and abusive parents? Is income maintenance fully utilized as a means of decreasing parental stress and preventing crisis? Third, scarce resources make coordination especially important in a rural community. Do law enforcement and social service work closely together in a trustful relationship on child abuse and neglect cases? Is the juvenile court seen as an important tool in helping families under stress? If there is a mental health center, is it engaged in outreach to prevent parental stress and family crisis? Is there close case coordination effected through a multi-disciplinary child protective team or less formal case conferences?

Availability of resources for the rural resident lead to a host of additional suggestions regarding outreach. Rural residents must be fully informed of the formal channels for child abuse reporting and be encouraged to use these channels. Use of mass media is indicated, as well as utilization of the informal networks which include town chairmen, ministers and social service clubs. Making the necessary remedial resources available to the rural resident may necessitate door-to-door canvassing, a countywide, crisis telephone line staffed by volunteers and outstationing services. Outreach may be extended by the development of a countywide committee on child protection.

Community organization is another essential ingredient in developing child protective services. As Dr. John Musick has forcefully pointed out, the community must be helped to have an impact on social policy.[10] In order for this to occur, the constituency of public agencies must be made accountable

---

[9]Ibid, page xv.
[10]Dr. John Musick, remarks at a workshop, "Social Work in the Twin Ports," University of Wisconsin-Superior, April 9, 1976.

for the needs of rural residents, rather than only for the control of funds. Citizen groups and informal advisory committees can play an important role in informing county boards of the needs of rural families and the human cost of not meeting those needs with adequate and available resources.

Effectively dealing with child abuse in a rural setting demands that we recognize the necessity for such aggressive means of combating the resident's isolation from services which prevent and treat parental stress. Failure to offer services to relieve family crises may lead to child abuse. Let's not be lulled by our pastoral surroundings--rural America requires innovative and aggressive efforts in child protection.

CHAPTER XI

YOUTH CRISIS SERVICES: SHORT-TERM COMMUNITY-BASED RESIDENTIAL TREATMENT

by Edmund T. Dimock

There is no consensus regarding methods for coping with the increase in juvenile crime in this country. However, there is agreement on the usefulness of prevention and diversion programs directed at the predelinquency level of activity.[1] Metropolitan areas offer a wide range of diversion services to keep predelinquent youths out of the juvenile justice system.[2] These programs range from shelters for runaways to centers that link youths with other community services.

Adolescents in need of diversion services come from a wide variety of backgrounds and present a range of behavioral problems, as indicated by the following examples:

> Mary, age 16, has lived with her married sister since her parents were killed in an auto accident 2 years ago. She is mature for her age, works part time and has her own automobile. The relationship with her brother-in-law is stormy. He believes Mary has too much freedom and is neglecting her commitments to the church. Recently Mary was picked up by the sheriff at a beer party. Her family felt this escapade was the "last straw" and refused to allow her to return home.
>
> Tom, 13, is the youngest of five children. His parents are marginally employed as harvest workers. The parents rarely have time for Tom, spending much of their time drinking and fighting with one another. Tom's resulting anger and frustrations were often ignored by the community and his parents. However, his budding aggressiveness was a concern to the school principal. Tom has been suspended three times this year for fighting. Finally, Tom exploded. He flew into a rage at school; windows were broken and desks overturned. Tom was taken from school by the police.

Neither Mary's nor Tom's situation is uncommon. In larger communities they probably would be referred to a program providing casework or other diversionary services. This is not so in many rural communities; problems of this nature are often viewed as the responsibility of law enforcement. The court is forced to assume responsibility, since resources for resolving family crises are not usually available locally.

---

1 ________. Delinquency Prevention Through Youth Development. Washington, D.C.: Government Printing Office, 1972, p. 3.
2 U.S. Department of Health, Education and Welfare. Better Ways to Help Youth: Three Youth Service Systems. Washington, D.C.: Government Printing Office, 1973.

This paper describes a program developed to serve small rural counties. It employs a community-based coeducational group home to provide voluntary diversion and short-term treatment services for adolescents.

Background

In 1972 Dr. Gerald Maguire, then Director of Mental Health Services for both Glenn and Butte Counties, California, proposed that mental health funds be used to provide a treatment alternative for adolescents coming into contact with the juvenile justice system. He was specifically concerned with predelinquent behavior, believing that most adolescent behaviors labeled "runaway" or "beyond parental control" are attempts by youths to resolve personal or family crises. He thinks treatment that allows youths to remain in the community can prevent involvement with the juvenile justice system.[3]

The Children's Home Society of California, a voluntary child welfare agency, saw merit in Maguire's proposal. After long negotiations involving many county and state agencies, it contracted with the two counties to provide diversionary treatment services for predelinquents referred by the local probation department. Youth Crisis Services, as the program is called, opened its first group home in Glenn County during February 1973. The program has since expanded into other northern California counties.

Diversion and Treatment Within the Community

The group home provides an alternative to jail or juvenile hall for youths, and a neutral environment where adolescents and their families are helped to resolve the problems that resulted in placement. In the latter function, the program: (1) provides distance between emotionally destructive parents and the adolescent; (2) decreases or eliminates the need for the youth to run away; (3) interrupts the family's pathological communication network; (4) provides an "emotional breather" for the adolescent; (5) provides a noncritical structured environment that allows change and fosters responsibility; and (6) removes the stress from parents.

Youth Crisis Services is a planned short-term service.[4] The maximum stay in the home is limited to 60 days. Most of the residents return home within 45 days.

The goal is to effect successful reintegration into the family system. This is best achieved in a community setting where contact between adolescent and family is easily maintained. Community settings help the youths maintain normal relationships with peers and enhance the residents' chances for success after return home.[5] Youth Crisis Services perceives the group home as

---

[3]Gerald Maguire. Personal communication.
[4]William J. Reid, and Ann Shyne. Brief and Extended Casework. New York: Columbia University Press, 1969, p. 3.
[5]Elery L. Phillips, et al. "Achievement Place: Modification of the Behavior of Predelinquent Boys Within a Token Economy," Journal of Applied Behavioral Analysis. IV, 1 (Spring 1971), p. 4.

an integral part of the community, with the staff performing a mediatory role between resident and community, involving the parents, and acting as liaison with schools.[6]

The residents interact with the community in many ways--purchasing groceries, attending school functions, going to the park and walking about the neighborhood. Such activities help the adolescents to maintain normal community ties. Successful interaction of residents with the community is dependent upon continuous intervention and interpretation by group home staff. Many of these activities are with the public schools, since slightly more than half of the adolescents referred to the program are considered problems in school.

Careful preparation during the development of the group homes resulted in initial community acceptance. Many of Stickney and Cupaiuolo's strategies for community residences were similar to those employed. These included selecting an appropriate neighborhood, not labeling the residence, filling the residence gradually and serving local people.[7] The initial acceptance eased the group home staffs' problems with the community, making it somewhat easier to resolve difficult situations when they arose.

Importance of a Consistent Program

Youth Crisis Services is predicated on a belief that individuals must get the opportunity to assume responsibility for their own behavior. Adolescents often perceive themselves as lacking control over many aspects of their lives, and fail to assume responsibilty for their actions. Also, parents often fail to see that they or their children have any available choices during periods of family conflict. Many adolescents never experience making a successful responsibility choice. Learning to make responsible decisions depends in part on experiencing situations that stress consistent expectations and opportunities. Consistency is an extremely important but difficult aspect of residential programs. Using a behavioral token economy as part of the milieu helps provide a consistent structure.[8]

Open communication is important to consistency. All parties, including the adolescent, must understand the treatment plans and goals for the adolescent and his family. In this process the case record is a valuable tool. Child care professionals make daily entries and the social workers record the results of family meetings. The adolescents have access to their own case records, the only condition being that a staff member be present to interpret or explain entries. Staff have learned to evaluate their statements prior to

---

[6]Fredrick Seidl, "Community-Oriented Residential Care: The State of the Art," Child Care Quarterly, III, 3 (1974), pp. 151-62.
[7]Patricia Stickney and Anthony Cupaiuolo. "From CRISP: Strategies for Community Residences," Child Welfare LV, 1 (January 1976), pp. 56-57.
[8]Phillips, et al., op.cit., p. 45.

committing them to the record.[9] Consequently, few judgmental statements or "labels" are noted.

Staff as a Mutual Support System

The group home is staffed by two child care professionals, a child care supervisor and a half-time social worker, the latter two being supervised by the program supervisor.

Primary child care responsibilities are shared by the two child care professionals, working on rotating three-day shifts. They are responsible for the day-to-day operation of the home and are the primary managers of the token economy. The child care supervisor works days and is responsible for the overall management of the home. The social worker has no supervisory responsibilities.

Youth Crisis Services de-emphasizes "professional" roles in an attempt to facilitate communication, in the belief that it occurs most freely between individuals perceiving themselves as nearly equal in status. The ideal model is a treatment team functioning as a mutual support system. This approach resulted in a team with working relationships based upon trust and cooperation. The social worker and the child care staff depend upon each other in many ways. Child care professionals develop expertise in child behavior and management techniques. The social worker is valued for skills with families and knowledge of community dynamics.

Unlike many residential settings that depend upon a social worker or other therapist for treatment, Youth Crisis Services views the adolescent's experience in the group home and the regularly scheduled family meetings as the essence of treatment. The child care professionals are much more than "substitute parents" or "babysitters" in this setting. They are involved with all aspects of the resident's life. Often, the quality of family meetings depends upon the input and participation of a child care professional. Many times, an adolescent's successful experience in school is directly related to the intervention of a group home staff member. In many respects, the child care professional's role is that of the "life space educator".[10]

Fostering Communication

Since success of the team approach is dependent upon clear communication, much of the inservice training is designed to increase staff's communication skills.

Communication within the program is also fostered through the use of regular, structured meetings. The child care professionals and the social

---

[9]Mary Lee Nicholson. "Child Care Practice and the Passions of Today: Some Propositions," Child Care Quarterly, IV, 2 (1975), p. 76.
[10]James K. Whittaker. "The Ecology of Child Treatment: A Developmental/ Educational Approach to the Therapeutic Milieu," Journal of Autism and Childhood Schizophrenia, V, 3 (September 1975), p. 234.

worker meet weekly to discuss residents, families and the behavioral management system. In addition, a structured two-hour meeting is held at every shift change to coordinate individual and team efforts and encourage program consistency.

The Token Economy

The token economy offers consistent criteria for the staff, and clear expectations for the residents. The system creates opportunities for residents to assume responsibility for their own behavior, and clarifies the relationship between act and consequence. The program stresses earned privileges rather than punishment or lost privileges, and has proved acceptable to the adolescents.

While defining expected behavior for all residents, the token economy becomes individualized by frequent use of behavioral contracts.[11] These individual agreements focus on specific problems such as school attendance or use of profanity.

The token economy, with feedback from the school, has helped improve school behavior of residents. Other situations also respond well to the token economy. For example, many adolescents resist attempts by parents or group home staff to impose curfews. In the group home a level system incorporated into the token economy allows the adolescent to earn "free time" up to the home's curfew, provided he demonstrates that he can use time away from the group home in an acceptable manner.[12]

The token economy is not a static structure; the residents are involved with the staff in trying to maintain a system that meets the needs of both. At regular group meetings, difficulties with the program are aired and adjustments or solutions discussed. Such meetings also help the youths develop peer communication skills.

Importance of Family Meetings

Koret sees family counseling as a major contribution to treatment of children in residential settings.[13] This is probably also true for adolescents whose attempts to emancipate themselves from their parents have brought them to the attention of the law.

Incidental interaction occurs frequently between group home staff and parents, but such contacts lack direction and rarely offer opportunities for

---

[11] Arthur Schwartz and Israel Goldiamond. Social Casework: A Behavioral Approach. New York: Columbia University Press, 1975, pp. 93-98.
[12] Margrit Meyer, E.S. Odom, and Bernice Wax. "Birth and Life of an Incentive System in a Residential Institution for Adolescents," Child Welfare LII, 8 (October 1973), p. 505.
[13] Sydney Koret. "Family Therapy as a Therapeutic Technique in Residential Treatment," Child Welfare LII, 4 (April 1973), p. 235.

intervention. For this, meetings must be structured and scheduled. Therefore, parents of each resident meet at least weekly at the group home. The meetings include family members, the youth in residence, the social worker and a child care professional.[14]

Family sessions focus on problems and are directed toward reuniting the adolescent with the family. Attention is paid to dysfunctional communication within the family. Improved family relationships are facilitated through contracts between various family members.[15] Behavioral contracts also serve to clarify or change maladaptive family "rules."

In many ways the family meeting is the key to success or failure of the diversion effort. Parents often have difficulty accepting any responsibility for their child's problems. However, they will usually participate as they suffer the "pain and strain" resulting from their child's behavior.[16]

Results

The Glenn County group home has been in operation since February 1973. Since then all appropriate adolescents have been diverted from the juvenile facility to the group home. (This averages 46 adolescents a year.) A comparison of the number of adolescents referred to the Glenn County Probation Department with the corresponding number of juvenile petitions filed in Superior Court for the period 1971 through 1974 shows a considerable reduction, from 11.7 percent to 6.2 percent.

The other Youth Crisis Services group homes have not been in operation long enough to evaluate their effectiveness. However, of the 394 adolescents receiving short-term services from all Youth Crisis Services group homes, only 10 percent were not placed successfully in a stable family setting after being in the group homes. Though the program is voluntary, only 17 percent of the families removed their children from the group homes prior to planned termination.

There are other indications that the program is successful. One probation officer said the program in her county has almost eliminated runaways. Another officer said, "We couldn't do our job without YCS's diversion efforts." One must also note the willingness of communities to tolerate the group homes.

Handler, discussing the difficulty of measuring the success of community programs, observed:

> One must remember too that these residential programs or their equivalents provide essential community services, no matter what

---

[14]Nada Finkelstein. "Family Participation in Residential Treatment," Child Welfare, LIII, 9 (November 1974), p. 575.
[15]James F. Alexander and Bruce Parsons. "Short-Term Behavioral Intervention With Delinquent Families: Impact on Family Process and Recidivism," Journal of Abnormal Psychology, LXXXI, 3 (1973).
[16]Whittaker, op.cit., p. 229.

their rates of success. Some youngsters simply refuse to live at home, some parents refuse to harbor certain children, and some youngsters are too difficult or disruptive for foster home care. Yet the community cannot abdicate responsibility for these minors.[17]

In the final analysis, the measure of success for a community-based residential treatment program may be the acceptance and support accorded it by the community.

---

[17]Ellen Handler. "Residential Treatment Programs for Juvenile Delinquents," Social Work, XX, 3 (May 1975), p. 222.

CHAPTER XII

DIMENSIONS OF YOUTH EMPLOYMENT IN RURAL AMERICA

by Kevin W. Lawless

Introduction

The focus of this chapter is to examine the multiplicity of vocational problems for rural youth and, more significantly, to offer models and initiatives for change. One such intiative that will be discussed is the creation of a youth-operated business which will be a community partnership model for rural areas.

Rural youths across the country are a silent, powerless and neglected population. Their future is being molded by the diminishing influence of rural tradition and the increased force of a tidal wave of urban and suburban humanity. In an unprecedented shift of living styles, the countenance of rural America is being altered and challenged at an alarming rate.

> For the first time in history, rural America is growing at a faster rate than urban Amerca. Some rural communities doubled in population between 1970 and 1976, and the trend continues. Hundreds of those communities grew at a rate two to three times as fast as the average growth for metropolitan counties during that period.[1]

Aside from the obvious burdens this growth creates for police and fire protection, other municipal services and schools, little attention has been paid to the effects--both short-term and long-term--on rural youth. What is indigenous to the socioeconomic tradition of rural America may be embodied in the response of rural youth to such changes and the character of that response will be determined by the network of family, educational, community, and private business and commercial influence.

Needs Specific to Rural Youth

The sociopsychological problems of adolescents and their search for acceptance, autonomy, self-esteem and identity are universal. The same problems for rual youth are exacerbated by many variables, the potentially greater of which is the rapidly changing structure of their communities. Other factors become more significant in light of this rapid change such as the availability and quality of professional services and accessibility to them. Another consideration is the bias of professionals who have been trained in urban areas; this becomes particularly significant when interacting with rural

---

[1]Robert Press, "Will Success Spoil Rural America?" Christian Science Monitor, 11 June 1979, p. 1.

youth. Compounding the problems of service delivery is the bias of federal funding formulas to urban areas.

> In addition to a lack of responses, there exists in many rural areas an attitude of benign neglect, characterized by the belief that youth and older Americans are a liability for the community--not useful, not competent, and not really belonging. The needs of these two specific groups to be competent, useful to the community, to be needed there--are the same as the general community--only their access and opportunities are different.[2]

Integration into the community is an essential developmental stage for youth. Effective solutions to the problems of rural adolescent drug abuse, delinquency, suicide, unemployment and the syndrome of their interrelationships must incorporate broadbased integration. This integration must involve the educational, therapeutic, civic and business elements of the community.

Employment as a Developmental Threshold

The opportunity to experience a positive vocational role outside of the family contributes to a healthy feeling of autonomy and independence for the adolescent. For many youth who are frustrated by the absence of meaningful work outlets, the search for autonomy is usually manifested by inappropriate behavior such as drug abuse, vandalism or running away. Unfortunately, vocational opportunities for youth are limited and the national unemployment rate is an embarrassment to a free enterprise system. The lack of meaningful, early vocational experiences contributes to poor work habits, inadequate training and low career aspirations. This, in turn, reduces the productivity of the country and fuels inflation as a burgeoning young work force must be trained and made employable.

An estimated 28 million youth will enter the labor force next year, an increase of over half a million. Federal youth employment programs, the majority of which are earmarked for urban areas, are targeted to reach only 1.7 million youth. It is evident that rural communities must be sensitive to the training and employment needs of their youth. Stimulation of meaningful work opportunities for youth will lend to the healthy development of rural adolescents and increase their capacity to influence the changing structures of their communities.

Logically, modern thought should be supportive of the concept of broad career exploration prior to a single occupational choice. However, educational institutions, which concentrate on single career choices offering a sufficient focus for organzing curriculum, contradict this assumption. For rural areas, there is even more of a linear focus based on philosophies rooted in the pragmatism of an early American agricultural society. The adaptability of

---

[2]Melody Tucker, "Critical Issues Facing Prevention Workers," U.S. Journal of Drug and Alcohol Dependency, (October 1978).

these philosophies to changing forces in the economic, political and educational realms without diluting rural tradition will be significant if rural youth are to become integrated into the larger community of the country. Indeed integration, or the ability to function within the political-economic power structure, will be critical to the future leaders of rural America.

Isolated rural youth who have poor attitudes and employment skills are hardly candidates for leaders. Their disenchantment pervades their entire social sphere. In a recent pilot study of juvenile delinquency,[3] it was concluded that two contributing factors were a lack of youth involvement in community decision making and a lack of youth investment in the community. Vocational opportunities, or the experience of completing a task, earning money and recognition outside of the family, is an integral step in the developmental process. It affords the adolescent an opportunity to be involved in a task-oriented, rewarding experience which engenders increased self-esteem, improved entry-level job skills and a new sensitivity to work and, ultimately, the community.

Youth Participation

Receiving a job through the school system or a local youth job placement service fulfills essential needs for youth other than monetary. However, one important aspect is neglected, which is youth involvement in the decision-making process of the community. Adult youth workers have developed a variety of vague terms to delineate youth as a class in society; such terms as "youth participation" and "youth advisory" are bandied throughout government regulations, direct service development plans and literature which advocates the value of youth's input into programs planned for them. Some are token attempts and labels while others are genuine in their commitment to empower youth. The Youth Advisory Committee of the National Network, an organization of runaway and youth serving programs, has attempted to clarify the distinctions. The Committee defines "youth participation and employment opportunities which involve youth in responsible, challenging action that meets genuine needs with opportunities for planning and/or decision-making, affecting others." Only through valid and genuine exercise of youth enablement can youth become decision makers and ultimately involved in the power structure of the community, whether it be urban or rural. For rural youth, the power structure is not as esoteric or removed as it is for urban youth; however, with little opportunity for exercise and access, it may just as well be.

Actualizing Youth Participation in the Operation of a Small Business

Creating true opportunities for youth participation will produce a spiral of positive responses from both youth and adults. Some youth exist in an impregnable ghetto, partially of their own design and partially of institutional and family neglect. Changing the way people perceive and relate to each other will ultimately mean engendering social change through positive means. This can be accomplished in rural and nonurban areas while at the same time

---

[3]James Forbes and Jeff Budd, "Outreach," Community Responses to Community Problems, 1979, p. 33.

addressing the employment needs of youth. Such approaches embody the strategy which is known as "prevention." Consequently, such prevention efforts mold into an efficient program instrument meaningful, realistic, yet challenging dimensions, while removing conditions in the community which contribute to youth alienation and under-involvement. The Tri-Town Council on Youth and Family Services, Inc., in Topsfield, Massachusetts, is attempting such a program by the operation of a youth-run business entitled "Restorations."

"Restorations" is a youth-operated enterprise involving the sale, repair and refinishing of used furniture. The purpose of the project is to give economically disadvantaged youth the opportunity to work and learn in the context of a small business. Overall program goals have been carefully outlined to remove barriers to youth career development and continually sustain their development within a supportive yet challenging environment. The characteristics of poor career and job development have their roots in adolescent work experience. One important objective of this project is to intervene early and effect a positive vocational experience. This positive vocational experience not only provides specific hands-on skill development, but integrates thereapeutic and vocational counseling to enhance ego enrichment and employability and to minimize attrition.

Another important dimension of this project is that it imparts an increased sense of autonomy and independence which are essential elements in the psycho-social, as well as vocational, development of the adolescent. This sense of autonomy is enhanced by the fact that not only will they be operating their own small business, but the future of that business will be contingent on their ability to perform successfully.

Specifically, the project employs eight adolescents, three of whom are full-time employees. Presently, there is also one full-time adult, the Project Director, who functions as a facilitator and technical advisor. The project currently receives subsidy for salaries and operational expenses and will eventually be totally self-sustaining. The full-time youth employees, who are high school drop-outs, receive tutorial assistance from the high school and all youth employees are awarded academic credit for their participation in the project.

Involvement and cooperation of local school systems is an essential component of the project. Making education relevant and meaningful is critical (the term relevance means actual experience or hands-on learning). "Restorations" is an excellent example of youth participation in off-campus learning experiences. The expanded environment of the classroom is dramatically more than a change in setting. It represents the realization that experience gained outside of the traditional educational setting can be as valid and often augments more traditional forms of learning. Hence, tradition is being replaced with relevance--a formula which may hold tremendous implications for rual America.

The opportunity to learn conversely creates the opportunity to teach. "Restorations" contracts with local artisans, craftsmen, business people and others for technical advice for the project. An important aspect of hiring these resource trainers is to recruit them from the community, which not only serves as a method of creating community awareness and publicity but, more significantly, engenders a spiral of interest and support from the adult community. The youth identify areas of need, recruit and interview trainers and contract with them for such technical advice as bookkeeping, advertising and furniture repair. Subsequently the youth have access not only to decision making backed with money, but are determining their own educational needs in a fashion which is meaingful to them.

The opportunity by which young people and adults with diverse skills and interests join in a common project which fosters mutual respect and contributes to the goal of self-sufficiency, addresses many needs for the rural community. "Restorations" is indeed a partnership between the youth and community. The success of the project to date has been dramatic. "Restorations" is well on its way to becoming a financially independent youth-operated business. But more importantly, "Restorations" is indicative of cooperative community efforts which are universal in their application. It also represents a last bastion--not of rigid traditionalism, but of a new partnership between the youth and adults which will adapt to the changing forces of society while embracing the economic and social values of rural America.

CHAPTER XIII

EDUCATIONAL JUSTICE FOR CHILDREN IN RURAL/NONMETROPOLITAN AREAS

by Joanne Jankovic

In the wake of movements toward explication of the rights of children and youth, one of the most difficult issues yet to be reckoned with is that which deals with the enforcement and implementation of legislative, judicial and administrative regulatory policy decisions, particularly at the state and local level. Little attention has been paid by governmental agencies historically to monitor compliance with new laws and regulations. As a result, several years often elapse before the impact of most progressive social legislation and law may be felt. Various factors make this particularly true in rural areas: (1) lack of governmental authority and/or concern to enforce compliance; (2) poor information programs; (3) lack of resources needed to implement mandated changes; and (4) failure of policymakers to take into consideration unique aspects of rural/nonmetropolitan areas.[1]

Despite this history, the federal government is becoming increasingly involved in providing national mandates to state governments to "humanize" their service delivery to the handicapped, to the aged and to individuals enmeshed in the juvenile/criminal justice systems. This is also true in the field of education, where a significant amount of attention has been given to the assurance and protection of children's rights by both courts and Congress; as a result, most educational practices are no longer solely under the scrutiny of state legislative bodies and educational agencies. Increased federal funding for education, along with regulatory guidelines which have to be met by school districts in order to receive such monies (as well as states' increased dependence upon those monies), have served to substantiate the federal government's serious role in education. Educational agencies, under federal requirements, must comply with mandates for free, appropriate education for all children and for administrative due process protections in educational placement planning, in matters of disciplinary exclusion from school activities, in parent access to children's educational records and in their involvement in their children's education. However, the extent to which public school administrators, teachers and other school personnel will recognize, uphold and carry out the spirit and objectives of such laws, is not known. It could be assumed that in those areas where there is a suburban/urban population base, more services, greater resources and wider availability of information channels (via newspapers and other media), there would be more awareness and concern over such issues than in rural areas. While rural areas at this time have more resources than ever before, they still endure unique problems: Fewer funds for services, greater geographic distances, less dense populations and a comparative lack of political influence in the games and resource allocation.[2]

School social workers, along with other agency personnel in rural areas, often find themselves in the dilemma of supporting progressive legislation on

---

[1]Roger Nooe and Joanne Jankovic, "The Future of Social Work Practice in Rural Areas," paper delivered at the 1979 Annual Program Meeting of the Council on Social Work Education, pp. 1-2.

[2]Ibid., p. 2.

the one hand, while they are constrained by the social and political realities common to most rural communities. For instance, the rural school practitioner is oftentimes the only social worker for a school district. The worker, isolated from professional peers, has little opportunity to use expertise, judgment or everyday common sense of other social workers in crucial situations.[3] Related to this is the fact that the worker may not have the opportunity to develop relationships with other school personnel. Assigned to more than one school, the school social worker is often recognized as an outsider--someone from the superintendent's office, thus making collegial relationship building difficult. Additionally, the rural practitioner, in approaching school administrators with issues of concern, often has to present a personal position with little or no other staff support. Despite the fact that the school social worker's job is often a function of legislative mandate, the worker may find him/herself continually compromised by the political forces that operate within the local school system. Furthermore, the very nature of the work undertaken by many rural practitioners makes advocacy efforts very difficult. Rural school social workers have a fair amount of community visibility, both in terms of their professional and personal lives. This is further complicated by community perceptions of the school social workers' role. Certain school systems and communities may place the limiting definitions of "truant officer" or "attendance worker" upon their workers; still in other areas, the school social worker is recognized as a major community resource, responsible for being involved in a wide variety of community issues--ranging from emergency housing relocation to serving as counselor to the juvenile court.

> In rural areas, kinship relationships and their effects on youth behavior are often stronger. Dealings among people in small communities are likely to be more personalized. However, creative recreational activites are often more scarce in rural areas. Access to a range of vocational training and career possibilities may be limited. Also, specialized services related to juveniles-family and youth counseling, professional law enforcement and judiciary services, group homes, and other rehabilitation aids--are not likely to be found in small towns and rural counties. Small local populations and tax bases often make it difficult to fund such services or to supply personnel who deal specifically with youth problems.[4]

Given scarce and scattered resources, and no professional support, the school social worker practicing in the rural setting is often required to serve as a major resource to programs outside the school which are continually penalized by poor funding support--the juvenile court, mental health, child welfare services.

The rural social services worker may find that established protections of client's rights, particularly confidentiality, privacy and due process for special populations, such as juveniles, are often compromised. The informal

---

[3]Richard Anderson and Joanne Jankovic, "Professional Education for Rural Practice," Social Work in Education, Vol. 1, No. 2, January, 1979, pp. 6-7.
[4]William Dan Bolton and David W. Brown, "Rural Juvenile Delinquency: Problems and Needs in East Tennessee," University of Tennessee Monograph, June 1978, p. 8.

structure of rural systems runs counter to the protection of such rights and leads to practices which are quite different from urban areas. For instance, federal requirements set forth by the Buckley Amendment regarding educational agencies' disclosure of information upon parental consent often go unregarded. Informal communication across agency lines as well as community familiarity with various clients of the school, welfare and court systems may serve to compromise the intent of regulations pertaining to confidentiality, access to information and requirements regarding exclusion, disciplinary action and consent to research. On the other hand this informal interchange may often work to the advantage of children and families in need of services, in that agencies may be willing to work together in order to pool scarce resources.

Secondly, the deinstitutionalization movement has found rural areas most in need of resource development. Adherence to administrative due process requirements often proves difficult when needed community alternatives to institutional care don't exist. This dilemma affects the provisions of individualized services to handicapped children in rural school systems under P.L. 94-142. Cost is a particular problem. Removing physical barriers, identifying children with handicapping conditions, providing needed educational opportunities is difficult in systems that have long suffered financial inequities, often failed to consolidate with other systems and have not had sufficient numbers of children needing specialized services to warrant the hiring of special education personnel.

Rural practitioners may also tend to have more involvement with law enforcement and juvenile justice agencies, due to the reliance upon the courts as one of the few major resources for children, despite the fact that a child may not have committed any offense. The courts are not as bound by heavy court caseloads normally encountered in urban areas, and may have more time on their hands to spend with cases. Certain states, studying problems resulting from legislative efforts to decriminalize status offenses, have noted that complaints often get lodged against children stemming from domestic problems, in order to get the child removed from home and placed in a temporary holding facility, such as a shelter or detention center.[5] In rural areas this may require that the child be placed in a lockup facility for an indeterminate period of time, removed from his or her community, school and peers. School social workers, while maintaining contact with children removed from home, will need to be aware of these issues and the fact that the child's involvement with the court process will nonetheless be stigmatizing and punitive.

However, despite the numerous problems we have identified in dealing with issues of assuring children's educational rights in rural areas, we do offer a number of suggestions that can be incorporated into everyday rural practice. It seems that as schools of social work focus more on specific fields of practice, emphasis on school-oriented practice must address the legal issues pertaining to school social work. Law and policy content should be designed to concentrate on issues pertaining to educational laws and policies

---

[5]Joseph DeJames, "Rural Response to Status Offender Legislation," paper presented at the First National Symposium on Rural Justce, June 20, 1979, pp. 9-11.

and related social legislation (as well as their origin), administrative due process mechanisms and other nonjudicial resolution systems, the role of the school social worker in proceedings requiring courtroom testimony, maintenance of records, and providing information input into child assessment procedures.

Practitioners already in the field should attempt to keep abreast of developments in related legal areas, such as changes in state juvenile codes, child welfare laws and the like. In rural areas, particularly, gaining access to information may often prove difficult. Nevertheless, even in the most isolated situations, there exists a pool of resources upon which the practitioner may draw. For instance, school social workers should be encouraged to participate in state professional organizations, not only to gain access to information that is available, but also to encourage these groups to provide judicial/legislative updates within their regular publications and other information resources.

Cooperative relationships need to be developed with those other agencies encountering similar problems in attempting to provide legal advocacy services to low-income clients. In many rural areas, legal services programs are becoming available and can be good resources for exchange, collaboration and support. A very encouraging movement among pre-paid legal services programs to develop consumer participation using client council groups makes even more resources available to the school social worker for problem identification, issue resolution and support. Those people who are members of client groups or other community organizations are often also parents. As a result, the network of relationships which extend from these groups to the schools can prove to be invaluable resources to the practitioner, thus removing some of the sense of isolation.

Rural school social workers, like their colleagues in other rural agency settings, will have to rely more and more on developing networks that cross geographic distance, agency lines, disciplines and levels of educational expertise. Networks are precisely the means by which the practitioner can avoid "reinventing the wheel." The sharing of problems and solutions in a collaborative sense will only serve to increase effectiveness. A situation which occurred in rural Georgia is a good example. A school system faced a serious attendance problem. Both teachers and students shared common negative attitudes regarding the worth of their educational experience. The school social worker, utilizing a community network consisting of the school board, the teachers, the parents, other agencies and the press, succeeded in mobilizing a local campaign to thwart this widespread indifference. Through publicity and working the local organizational network, the learning environment was improved. Hence, individual problems decreased and a much healthier organizational environment began to develop.

Over and over again experience has proven the effectiveness of network building. However, the questions for the practitioner are much more specific. Whom do you approach and how? In regard to purely informational access questions, the approach is simple and direct. One goes to the legal aid office and asks for briefs, court decisions and the like. In a more organizational sense, it is imperative to approach other groups, through information workshops, and to welcome their input to the schools. Even in rural areas, utilizing an educational approach, one can begin to sensitize lawyers, agency personnel, civic groups, political parties, and the general community to problems affecting students' lives. The increased involvement of these individuals and groups can serve to give the rural practitioner support in his or her own advocacy efforts. It is also extremely important to note that the worker in the rural setting must go to even greater lengths to insure that clients--the parents and the children, understand legal issues and rights, and more importantly, are deeply involved in efforts to support protections of their rights and their children's rights. Social workers cannot do it alone and need the awareness and involved support of the parents and children. If there is no direct parent constituency group such as a PTA, then the worker has two choices--either he/she approaches other established community groups or devotes time and resources to organize parental input and understanding. Whatever the approach, the message for effectiveness is clear. The social worker must utilize community resources to gain needed legal, legislative and agency knowledge; at the same time he/she must be willing to use these resources in dealing with basic problems of educational justice. Self-contained, insulated programs such as public educational institutions, not privy to community support, are doomed to fail if left in the hands of a few. For we must remember that the schools are not purely educational institutions. They are also an established, sanctioned means of social control. As Costin asserted:

> The present system of public education...serves in a variety of ways the less openly acknowledged purpose of social control. Through tests, curricular tracking, judgments about pupil behavior and other means, the school sorts out and distributes pupils according to age, sex, race and fitness for certain occupations and societal positions, but the process is the same for all groups. The schools frequently classify children and young persons for failure as they persuade them to see themselves as the school defines them.[6]

Educational justice for children, whether or not they live in cities, suburbs or rural areas is of significant importance. Especially in the more isolated areas, it is the responsibility of the school social worker to gain access to information pertaining to issues of rights, due process and requirements of progressive educational and social legislation and to make it available to the schools. It is only through this community mobilizing effort that rural communities can provide input into the educational process. Awareness, input, and involvement are essential ingredients to assure justice within the school setting.

[6]Lela Costin et. al., "Barriers to Social Injustice," Social Work Practice and Social Justice, Bernard Ross and Charles Shireman, eds. (Washington, D.C., National Association of Social Workers, 1973), p. 3.

Part IV

CONCLUSION

Introduction

Our final chapter by Dr. David W. Brown, International Professor of Agricultural Economics and Rural Sociology at the University of Tennessee, Knoxville, represents an assessment of the difficulties encountered in making decisions which impact rural communities in the attempt to improve juvenile services. He suggests that some basic principles from economics can be useful in making best use of scarce resources and elaborates a problem-solving framework which takes into consideration the need to assess potential consequences of various policy program choices. Most importantly, he emphasizes the need that resources must be used wisely and in a careful consideration of all realistic alternatives.

CHAPTER XIV

THE ECONOMICS OF CONCERN AND COMPASSION: APPLICATIONS TO RURAL JUSTICE

by David W. Brown

Let me start by telling what this presentation is not about. It is not going to barrage you with all sorts of facts and figures. Nor does it seek to impose a dollar value on human life, personal dignity or other intangibles that are so important to rural justice. Nor will this be an attempt to impress profesional peers with manipulations of mathematics, supply-and-demand curves and such that economists love to flouirsh.

What my presentation does seek to do is suggest a framework--an orderly way of thinking...a diagnostic perspective--that can be useful when planning actions and weighing alternatives related to the area of rural justice.

Healthy doses of dedicated fervor and pressure to move ahead quickly are indeed essential if headway is to be made. But these energies can be wasted if not carefully husbanded. Everything can't be done at once. Helping one group may have to be at the expense of neglecting others. Tough decisions have to be made about how to use scarce funds, time and talents. Priorities have to be set. Efficient approaches need to be sorted out from the ineffecient. Whether the concern is with a multi-million dollar national program or simply using one's own time wisely at the local level, there are usually many options when it comes to deciding what to do, how to go about it, where to start first, how fast to proceed, whom to involve and when to let go. The very urgency of the need to correct inequities and shortsighted practices makes it crucial that available resources be used wisely and that careful choices be made among the viable alternatives.

An Example--Alternatives for Dealing with Rural Juvenile Delinquency Problems

Let me illustrate with some of the decision-making issues associated with rural juvenile delinquency problems.

Recently we completed a study of local delinquency problems, programs, and felt-needs in the 15-county area surrounding Knoxville (Note 1). This area has several towns and cities with healthy economic growth and convenient access to social services. But it also includes a number of small communities in outlying rural settings where county tax bases are small, outlets for youth limited and professional help scarce. Delinquency problems have been increasing. Many places in this East Tennessee area have not had specialized facilities or personnel to deal with delinquency, status offenses and other youth problems. Though most local officials wish it could be otherwise, youth in metropolitan settings of East Tennessee have often been handled in an adult-like manner or sent to institutions elsewhere in the state.

We asked 51 persons, concerned at least part-time with rural juvenile problems at local or area levels (judges, law enforcement personnel, personal counselors and school officials), to indicate the kinds of local services deserving special attention or improvement in the future. Their responses highlighted: professional counseling referral services; juvenile probation services; detention facilities especially designed for youth; recreational facilities and programs; training for local officials and volunteers concerned with juvenile problems; use of group homes and halfway houses; foster care programs; help to youth in getting jobs; and specialized juvenile courts with adequate support staff.

Think about some of the issues and alternatives faced by a rural community or county with a small population and income base if it is to use its limited resources effectively toward the improvement of such juvenile services. Questions like the following need to be addressed:

> At the broad strategy level, should emphasis be on (1) prevention of delinquency problems, or (2) improved local law enforcement and adjudication processes, or (3) better treatment and rehabilitation services for youth and families who have problems?
>
> Within any one of these three categories, what specific facilities, services, or programs should receive priority?
>
> Are there ways to combine certain services in the locality (e.g., adult and youth counseling or cooperation with the school system) so that there will be cost savings or better results?
>
> Can there be cost savings or better results by pooling efforts with neighboring counties or by cooperating with area-wide undertakings, or by using specalized services in nearby urban centers? (Often, local youth services are more convenient and personalized, but they are expensive.)
>
> How far should the locality go in making use of help from state and federal sources? (Such programs offer access to funds, facilities and specialized professionals that individual rural places could never provide on their own. But participation may be at the cost of burdensome compliance and matching-fund requirements.)
>
> In dealing with local delinquency problems, are there ways to draw upon "free" help from volunteers, churches, civic groups, etc.? (Such involvement could also be a way to rekindle the spirit of neighborliness and mutual caring that historically has been an important part of rural living but that is in danger of disappearing.)

Similarly, people at district, state and federal levels face many issues related to the alleviation of juvenile problems in rural areas. For example:

> What basis to use for deciding how to divide program funds among various places? Seriousness of the problem? Scarcity of local resources? Local capability and enthusiasm? Effects on future political support for the program? Or what?
>
> Should emphasis be on immediate impacts or on lasting, long-term results?
>
> Should emphasis be on comprehensive services and facilities in major towns and cities? Or on decentralization and ready access by people in outlying places?

In trying to upgrade juvenile services, to what extent should there be emphasis on the "carrot" approach (leadership education, cost-sharing, voluntary participation) as distinct from the "stick" approach (insistence that all places meet certain standards or follow certain procedures)?

Public officials and agency personnel aren't the only ones who face tough decisions. Groups trying to influence legislation and public opinion related to juvenile problems also face some tough decisions about how best to channel their lobbying and educational efforts:

Where to concentrate efforts? At grassroots constituency levels? In state and national legislative circuits? Via participation in agency advisory boards? Or what?

How best to reach the intended audience? Group meetings, one-on-one sessions with key influentials, mass media or what?

How much change to press for at any one time?

When to make the big educational or lobbying push? And for how long to continue the campaign?

Concepts From Economics Can Be Helpful

The examples that I've given stem from juvenile delinquency concerns. But many similar choices crop up when tackling other rural justice needs. In coming to grips with such issues--whether they are broad policy questions or the nitty-gritty decisions of the individual program worker or volunteer--there are several concepts from the field of economics that can be helpful in organizing one's thinking.

Many basic economics texts would lead one to believe that economics deals with only big business, profits, inflation control, trade, price forecasting and such. But its conceptual underpinnings carry much broader implications. In fact, it was concern for poverty and human injustices that led many of the early economic theorists to formulate their theories. The following definition (Note 2) of economics sums it up nicely:

> Economics is the study of the behavior of man and his institutions as they relate to the allocation of scarce resources.

Economics has a long way to go in fulfilling this defined task but, as those who deal with rural justice will testify, the focus on how to use scarce resources effectively is certainly a relevant one, and the need to account for the realities of human concerns, responses, and institution is indeed important.

Let's brush away the cobwebs from some basic economic decision concepts and think how they can be applied to rural justice concerns:

1. Diminishing added returns--the frequent reality that, while some resources which intensify or upgrade an undertaking may have a high payoff,

there will be a point where added inputs will do little to further help performance. This applies to human services programs and voluntary efforts just as much as it does to factory and farm production. For example, a few group homes may do a lot of good, but a point of oversaturation can be reached.

2. Opportunity cost--the need, when investing time and funds in one undertaking, to consider what is being neglected by not using those resources in other ways. Tying up local funds in law enforcement equipment may mean less funds for human services personnel training. Establishing a new state institution for delinquent youths is likely to be at the expense of alternative living facilities and counseling services back home where the kids run into problems. And so on.

3. Complementary relationships. There may be ways to combine or coordinate two or more undertakings so that each one helps the other. Sometimes one plus one can equal three! For example, cooperation between counselors in the juvenile court system and the local schools can do much to enhance each other's effectiveness.

4. Input substitution--the reality that there may be more than one way to provide certain services and that cost effectiveness may be an important consideration. For example, a locality might compare the costs of running its own mental health clinic vs. paying a private clinic to held needy cases as required. Also relevant is the need for flexibility to allow agencies to move ahead in the best way possible. How often is the case where there was some slack funding in the overall budget, but a freeze on travel prevented staff from visiting local offices or participating in useful training activities?

5. Size economies. It's not always true, but for many services and facilities there can be significant cost savings by running one large operation instead of several little ones. In sparsely populated rural counties there may be too few cases to fund a comprehensive mental health center or a juvenile court facility very effectively; there may be worthwhile economies of size by pooling efforts with nearby counties. At the same time, it is possible to over-centralize. Relying on one large facility or service network can result in added administrative layers and travel expenses that more than offset the gains.

6. Locational considerations. Where should the institutions which help rural people be placed? "Location theory" and other concepts of regional economics tell us that, from an efficiency viewpoint, few services would be based in small rural towns and villages; comprehensive facilities and agency headquarters serving a region would be in major centers, and branch offices or facilities would be in middle-sized towns or cities. From the standpoint of politics and local access to jobs, there may be justification for spreading some major installations around, rather than concentrating everything in the same center. But where there is a proposal to establish a regional prison or specialized medical facility in a small hamlet off the beaten track, it behooves one to take a close look at how the remote location and separation from companion services will affect results. Also, careful consideration has to be given to administrative boundaries; it may or may not make sense, when establishing new programs, to follow traditional county or agency district lines.

7. Comparative advantage. Applied to rural justice undertakings, this economic concept calls attention to the need for effective use of training and experience. Often we see social workers and law enforcement personnel bogged down in routine paper work that clerical staff could handle. Likewise, it increasingly appears that the skills of doctors, dentists and lawyers--so scarce in many rural areas--could be used to fuller advantage if there was encouragement by semi-professionals.

8. Fixed and variable costs. When initiating or expanding a rural justice undertaking, it's the added (out-of-pocket) costs that count. The accounting practice of prorating all costs may not be appropriate when making such decisions. For example, attaching a legal counselor to a senior citizens' center may require funds for a salary, a desk and some travel. But no additional funds for office space or secretarial help are likely to be needed if use can be made of excess space and secretarial time already available at the center. However, it works the other way, too. When considering elimination of a service, only those cost items that would change would enter the decision.

9. Direct and indirect effects. Rural justice undertakings may have important "multiplier" or "ripple" effects that should be taken into account. A new mental health clinic, if successful, may serve as a demonstration that stimulates groups in other rural places to organize similar clinics. There may be important intangible spinoffs which inspire a fresh spirit of hope, cooperation, endeavor and spark other important improvements in the community.

10. The time value of costs and benefits. Some rural services (for example, adding more sheriff patrols to curb vandalism) have relatively immediate effects but may not address the heart of a problem. Alternative approaches (better recreational and vocational outlets for rural youth) may have more lasting impacts but have high "front end" costs and require some time before results are seen. People (politicians especially?) prefer the option that has the quickest payoff; the longer they have to wait, the more they tend to "discount" future results. For a slow payoff alternative, decision makers will often have to be convinced to take a long-term view and be shown that the overall effects are considerably greater than with the quick payoff alternative.

11. Risk considerations. Given two options--a risky approach and a sure bet--most people would choose the sure bet if the most likely outcomes are about the same. If a risky line of action is being proposed, one may have to show that a) spectacular results could be achieved; b) the consequences won't be too bad or irreversible if things go wrong; and/or c) there are ways to reduce the odds of bad results (such as trying an innovative program on a pilot basis at first).

12. Efficiency vs. equity and freedom. Economists are generally preoccupied with efficiency--either achieving as much as possible with a given set of resources or getting something done for the least cost. Being efficient is a vital consideration if headway is to be made in conserving the rural environment, protecting the rights of disadvantaged rural people, opening new opportunities to improve life quality and reaching various other goals. But being efficient sometimes comes at the expense of neglecting certain needy

groups, moving ahead without involving those affected in decisions, or of imposing stiff requirements for compliance without much opportunity for recourse. These two issues--how much freedom to sacrifice and how much inequity to tolerate--are at the heart of the debate related to rural justice needs and solutions. Economics can't supply the answers [that gets into value judgements and the consensus-building process], but it can call attention to tradeoffs between efficiency and equity or freedom concerns.

Putting Things Together in a Problem-Solving Framework

One or more of the economic concepts just mentioned will usually enter the picture when dealing with a specific rural justice issue or program. But as a point of departure in coming to grips with key decisions, a more cohesive framework is needed. Many people find it useful to approach things in the following manner:

Step A. Pinpoint the problem that you're trying to solve or the direction in which you want to move.

Step B. Diagnose the reasons why the problem persists or why more progress isn't being made.

Step C. Identify the viable alternatives for alleviating the situation and predict the likely results of each.

Step D. Weigh the alternatives and decide what to do using appropriate criteria.

Underlying all four of these steps is the need to take into account the "task environment"--relevant elements of the geographical, historical, cultural, technological, political, institutional and ideological settings in which the actions being considered are to take place.

This framework can be useful whether the decision at hand is large or small and whether the accompanying analysis is complex or simple. Let me elaborate.

Step A. While broad rhetoric has its place in generating public concern, there comes a time when an undertaking has to be defined more sharply and trimmed down to manageable size. Which specific rural health problems are you going to tackle first? And where? When you talk about "juvenile problems," do you mean delinquents, status offenders, the abused and neglected, or whom?

A problem doesn't exist unless there is a gap between the existing situation and some aspired goal. But it isn't always easy to pin down these goals, especially where intangibles like individual rights, community spirit and environmental aesthetics are involved.

Sometimes means and ends become confused or hard to distinguish. For example, the right to work beyond 65 may be in itself a source of satisfaction to older people and not just a way to augment income or keep busy. Heated opposition to a court reform proposal may make winning that particular battle the main preoccupation at the expense of a broader objective of more equity in the legal system.

Step B. It is important to look beneath the symptoms and identify the underlying causes--for example, the way many juvenile behavioral problems apparently are traced to difficulties in the family.

In identifying the causes, it's important to distinguish between those one can and cannot do something about. Some sources of rural injustice can be tackled right away. Others require legislative actions. Still other obstacles can't be alleviated until another generation is educated and basic changes in human attitudes have taken place.

Step C. It is important to predict program performances and human responses that are actually likely to take place-not what would happen ideally if everything went well. Many "slippages" can enter the picture at various points of conceiving, gaining acceptance, mobilizing and completing a rural justice undertaking. At the same time, if one worries unduly about all that can go wrong, nothing would ever get started. As economist Albert Hirschman (Note 3) has pointed out, there often is a "hiding hand" effect in which obstacles and setbacks stimulate fresh ideas and vigor that otherwise would never have appeared.

In predicting responses to various proposed actions, it helps to view things through the eyes of organizations, the specific communities or individuals being effected. If they are expected to respond in the intended way, three elements are necessary: (1) They need to have adequate knowledge about the proposed change; (2) they need to have financial, organizational and legal capability to make the change; and (3) they need to have adequate inducement of either positive incentives or negative penalties. Where a law or regulation is involved, often it is not the severity of the penalty that matters so much as the uncertainty of its enforcement.

Step D. Depending on the circumstances, review of a rural justice problem, its causes and the remedial possibilities can have several outcomes:

1. One can do nothing and wait for more opportune circumstances.

2. One can defer the decision until better information is at hand.

3. One can select a single alternative and proceed.

4. One can establish priorities and move ahead in sequence as time and funds become available.

5. One can select a combination of actions that either a) complement one another and enhance total performance; or b) diversify efforts and reduce the odds of everything going wrong.

In arriving at such choices, any of several decision "models" may be appropriate for pulling together and assessing the relevant information [See Table 1].

Finally, a word about how the underlying task environment can temper the use of resources in planning and implementing rural justice undertakings.

Sometimes the mood of a locality, state or the nation as a whole can affect how and when it's best to do things. At the moment, the U.S. seems

TABLE 1

Some Decision Models That Can Be Applied to Rural Justice Undertakings

Decision model	Example
Maximizing achievement of a dominant objective within the bounds of certain constraints. [Benefit-cost analysis can be a useful decision and where long-term choices are involved.]	Providing as many rural families as possible with convenient access to mental health services without raising local taxes very much.
Minimizing the cost or negative consequences of achieving a certain level of performance.	Finding the least expensive way of providing people in remote places with emergency medical services.
Weighing the trade-offs between two or more competing objectives. [The choice depends on value judgements, deciding how heavily to weight each objective.]	Deciding whether to centralize regional probation counseling services. Basing the counselors in one central place may be more cost-efficient and make it easier to attract good professionals, but result in less understanding of local situations.
Minimizing the risk of failure. [There are various models for decision making under uncertainty that one can turn to.]	Sometimes the dilemma of a new program which still needs to gain public acceptance and regular budget support. Possible answers include diversifying activities, avoiding high-risk or irreversible options and trying things out on a small-scale pilot basis.
Minimizing the consequences of active opposition. One can usefully draw upon the "game theory" concepts used by military and business strategists.]	Possible need of advocates of juvenile justice reform and deinstitutionalization to take into account the counter-reactions of groups who resist such changes.
Satisfying--doing enough to make reasonable progress, keep problems from getting worse, avert crises and give balanced attention to the needs of various groups.	Sometimes this is about all an overburdened, multifaceted human services agency or law enforcement system can hope to do. Flexibility of response to special needs may be an important ingredient.

to be going through a "conservative" cycle in which there is pressure to reduce government spending, come down harder on deviant behavior and worry less about the disadvantaged. However, some observers predict that this will reverse itself and that by the mid-1980's there will be a more "liberal" mood. If so, this implies that it may be expedient for social reformers to "lie low" for a while--to tackle changes in a more incremental fashion as opportunities open up--to concentrate on improved public understanding of the problems and remedies--to develop and test fresh ideas that might be employed on a wider scale when the mood is right.

A second example of the importance of taking the task environment into account has to do with the characteristics of nonmetropolitan localities. Some rural communities continue to be very traditional, composed mostly of families and leaders who have been there a long time, homogeneous because most are in farming or mining and have similar ethnic background, isolated and perhaps reluctant to accept outsiders or new ideas unless they are strongly endorsed by local leaders. Other communities have experienced important changes, have had urbanizing influences and are more heterogeneous and less cohesive. In East Tennessee, one finds in many counties a diverse mixture of farmers, family members who work in nearby towns, urban professionals who have sought country life and retired persons who have returned or migrated from other places. Tourism and recreational attractions are dominant elements in some counties. Still other counties--those near growing metropolitan centers--consist mostly of bedroom communities inhabited by new arrivals who have few links to one another and who take little interest in community affairs unless their own children or subdivisions are directly affected. These differences among localities carry implications for rural justice undertakings--the problems that need priority attention, the best way to generate public understanding and acceptance of new proposals, the pace at which to move ahead, the funding potentials and the extent to which local leadership and volunteer help can be utilized.

A third example of how the task environment affects things relates to underlying ideologies, values, ethics and concepts of justice. Some societies have accepted processes of reform which greatly curb individual freedom and deal with certain groups harshly. Other societies (the U.S. included) have placed great emphasis on not retracting freedoms or economic advantages already gained, e.g., the reluctance of many communities to impost strict zoning or to expropriate land without compensating the owners. The processes of urbanization and industrialization which are affecting many of our rural areas make it important to take a fresh look at these underlying values and ideologies. There will be more disagreement between different groups about how best to use scarce land areas. Increasingly, what one person does may have adverse effects on others, e.g., water pollution below a strip mining area or the traffic congestion along a highway created by unrestrained commercial development (these are what economists call "externalities"). In the future, we shall probably have to give up certain rights and freedoms in order to retain others. Which freedoms to sacrifice and which to protect is likely to be at the heart of many issues and decisions in decades to come.

Conclusion

The ideas discussed here may seem "textbookish" and basic. Of course in real life programs don't evolve that neatly and there may not be time to do much diagnosis. Also, allocating scarce resources among competing alternatives is not the only consideration when tackling rural problems; other diagnostic perspectives are equally important. For instance, sociology provides key insights into legitimizing new ideas, diffusing information, organizing communities and motivating people. The field of "institution building" calls attention to the internal characteristics and external linkages that are especially important if new undertakings are to become self-sustaining. From law and political science we can acquire valuable insights about pre- and post-legislative processes.

Nonetheless, taking time to examine what we're doing from the viewpoint of economic realities and resource use effectiveness carries implications for persons in a variety of roles:

> For legislators, these economic decision-making considerations suggest the danger of overprescribing standards, funding formulas and methods of approach. Some flexibility in meeting diverse local situations and changes is needed.
>
> For administrators, wise decisions will not be made unless they encourage grassroots feedback about problems, resource constraints and likely impacts on specific groups.
>
> For advisory board members and advocacy groups, this economic view highlights the need to pinpoint problems and causes in specific terms, to offer viable solutions and not to become wedded to a particular course of action.
>
> For the individual program worker or volunteer, these concepts are useful to remember when mapping out day-to-day activities. Better decisions about how to use one's own time and effort can add up!
>
> For professional analysts, the resource allocation perspective shows the need for better concepts, facts and methodology to help diagnose rural justice problems, identify possibilities and assess future outcomes. Mere description of what has happened in the past will not do the job.

One could in a presentation like this, call attention to the useful refinements of economic theory, e.g., the field of "welfare economics" and quantitative techniques, e.g., linear programming. But no amount of analytical sophistication and research funding will help if orderly decision-making approaches are not an integral part of everyday thought. This boils down to three basic questions that we need to keep in mind.

1. Does the proposal really get at the problem and is it workable?

2. Will it have the purported effects?

3. It is the best way?

NOTES

1. For a report of this study, see William Dan Bolton and David W. Brown, Rural Juvenile Delinquency: Problems & Needs in East Tennessee, Tennessee Agricultural Experiment Station Bulletin 580, June 1978.

2. This definition was used by Professor Dale Dahl of the University of Minnesota in a paper given at the Economic Research Conference on U.S. Food System Regulation, Airlie House, Virginia, April 17, 1979.

3. See Albert O. Hirschman, Development Projects Observed (Washington, D.C.: Brookings Institution, 1967), especially Chapter 1.